I0005110

TABLE OF CONTENTS

DISCLAIMER AND TERMS OF USE AGREEMENT:

(Please Read This Before Using This Book)

This information is for educational and informational purposes only. The content is not intended to be a substitute for any professional advice, diagnosis, or treatment.

The authors and publisher of this book and the accompanying materials have used their best efforts in preparing this book.

The authors and publisher make no representation or warranties with respect to the accuracy, applicability, fitness, or completeness of the contents of this book. The information contained in this book is strictly for educational purposes. Therefore, if you wish to apply

Introduction – The Internet Can be Your Best Friend or Your Worst Enemy

 Hello and thank you for purchasing my book. I am Dr. Treat Preston and as a behavioral scientist, I usually write about the human condition but not this time. Yes, one of the most horrible human conditions is the seemingly endless pain a person can afflict on another human being and as a Senior Forensics Investigator, I have seen some of the most horrible humanity afflicted on other human beings to a point where the demons just won't go away and will be with me forever.

This book is about a subject that is so pervasive worldwide that it now afflicts millions upon millions in every country and region of the world. I am speaking about reputation slander where an individual or company is attacked viciously online with the goal of literally destroying them individually or corporately and the success ratio is very high because it is human nature to love a scandal – fabricated or real.

What is unusual about this book is that it is NOT a human mind book that I often write about but I have included in the Prologue "Laying a Proper Foundation" with a description of "The Mechanism of the Human Mind" which describes the behavioral science of why people do the things they do and I feel it is necessary for my readers to understand how evil permeates the human mind and why people attack and hurt other people.

My goal in writing this book is to not only make you aware of the problem but also show you how to prevent it and repair the damage if it has already occurred in your life.

The very first thing to understand that there is no such thing as privacy on the Internet unless you take steps to guard your privacy.

Secondly, at any given time SOMEONE or SOME ENTITY is watching your every move on the Internet. Yes – ALWAYS!!! Now many of them are harmless such has behavioral marketing sites looking to study your browsing and buying habits but watch they do!

I am going to show you how this occurs and how to protect yourself. We all have been made aware of the NSA wiretaps and intrusions into our cell phone records, text messages and voice calls all in the name of national security. But as the record shows, where was the NSA when it came to preventing the Boston Marathon bombings? So is this a very clever excuse to spy on the American public or is it something that is truly necessary? I will give the facts and allow my readers to decide. And decide you must because your very future is at stake and this is a problem that isn't going to go away.

Throughout this book I will be drawing from my company's series of forensics books as follows:

Cyber Crime/Cyber Forensics

Confessions of a Child Predator
http://www.amazon.com/dp/B007BB97KU

Child Watch
http://www.amazon.com/dp/B0095K1P3M

Cyber-Daters Beware
http://www.amazon.com/dp/B006J9T4NA

Cyber Protect Your Business
http://www.amazon.com/dp/B0095JEAYY

ForensicsNation Bushwhacker Program
http://www.amazon.com/dp/B007I9AHVS

ForensicsNation Catalog
http://www.filefactory.com/f/d3eac5e74de46025

ForensicsNet™/ForensicsLab™
http://www.amazon.com/dp/B00IMLCAPC

Hackers and Crackers
http://www.amazon.com/dp/B00EXQ0HDC

Judgment Not Included
http://www.amazon.com/dp/B00CPRSQ3E

Protecting Yourself from Cyber Crime
http://www.amazon.com/dp/B0095J3EIW

Sleeping with Guns
http://www.amazon.com/dp/B00CS1IBZU

Stealing You
http://www.amazon.com/dp/B00778TT6E

The Mind Of a Con Man
http://www.amazon.com/dp/B00CO2BQHI

Was Sandy Hook a Hoax?
http://www.amazon.com/dp/B00BFSM8IS

Why Women Should Not Use Online Dating Services
http://www.amazon.com/dp/B006J9EMH8

You Can Run But You Cannot Hide
http://www.amazon.com/dp/B006JLVZC6

As a Senior Forensics Investigator I have resources and intelligence available to me that the average person simply does not have access to and because of this most people merrily go about their lives oblivious to the dangers lurking on the net and are totally blindsided when they are attacked.

To begin, let's address what reputation slander truly is and why another person or entity does this. Reputation slander is when someone or some entity posts malicious lies and innuendo on the Internet about an individual or company with the sole purpose of destroying the person or entity.

The why behind they do this is best addressed in the Prologue. Basically a person gravitates to the desires, emotions and will of their psyche. Because of this a person bypasses their intellect and uses their basic primeval instincts of hatred, wrath, greed, sloth, pride, lust, envy, and gluttony. This occurs in all types of businesses and individuals but is especially used against book publishers and successful authors, successful people in general, politics, entertainment, successful businesses, and much more.

As an aside, here is something that will really knock you down. In my company, ForensicsNation, I am presently assigned to the sexual predators unit. Look at the chart below. I am located in Northern California in the town of Auburn but my company is in Cedar, City, Utah which is a small community of 33,000 people. In this tiny town there are 37 registered sex offenders. Now these are

REGISTERED offenders, which means they have served their prison time and are under the supervision of their parole or supervised release officers. As an investigator I do not worry about registered sex offenders; the ones I go after are the ones that are released and do not register and simply disappear into the woodwork. Would you like to bet your hard money on what are the odds they will commit another offense? DON'T!

SEXUAL OFFENDERS
The Nationwide Safety Network .com

http://www.sexualoffenders.com/

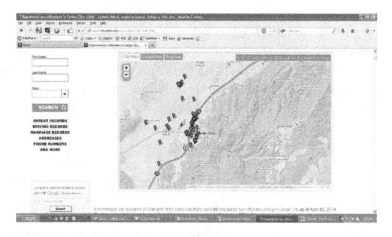

The purpose of bringing this topic up is to demonstrate to you one type of cybercrime that is so pervasive and dangerous. Sexual addiction cannot be cured so the best law enforcement can do is supervise the sexual offenders once they are released and with a recidivism rate of 96% for sexual offenders (THIS IS HOW MANY SEXUAL OFFENDERS COMMIT ANOTHER CRIME AND ARE

RETURNED TO PRISON) you can see that the problem is pretty bad.

Here is another statistic that will floor you - If you were to take all of the law enforcement agencies in the world today and combine them with all of the private companies such as ForensicsNation, all of us combined wouldn't even make a dent in cybercrime not to mention all other types of crime. Is that scary or what? So what is the answer? In one word – PREVENTION! By making you aware of what is out there and showing you how to protect yourself, this is the only way to crawl on top of the problem.

My company has produced a FREE Online Public Awareness Video. It is 56-minutes in length and I highly recommend you watch it. Go here and sign up to watch it online:

http://www.AddMeInNow.com

Okay, so move onto the next section and learn about the human mind including the criminal mind and why you and other people do the things you and they do…

As stated, I want to begin this book by offering an insight into the human mind as seen by behavioral science research. By doing this, I will lay a proper foundation to what I am about to teach.

The Mechanism of the Human Mind

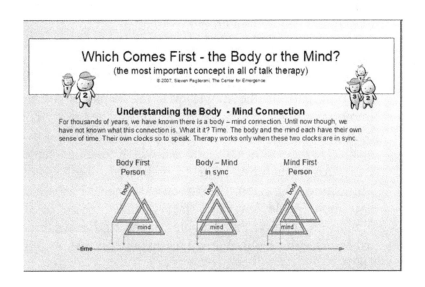

Which Comes First - the Body or the Mind?
(the most important concept in all of talk therapy)
© 2007, Steven Paglierani, The Center for Emergence

Understanding the Body - Mind Connection

For thousands of years, we have known there is a body – mind connection. Until now though, we have not known what this connection is. What it it? Time. The body and the mind each have their own sense of time. Their own clocks so to speak. Therapy works only when these two clocks are in sync.

| Body First Person | Body – Mind in sync | Mind First Person |

Prior to the fall of man into sin as described in the Garden of Eden, man's spirit was hooked to God's infinite spirit. There was no death because God's spirit is infinite. Man is the only animal on earth that shares the eternality nature of God. The subject of eternal life has been a heated topic of man from the beginning of our existence.

In Greek mythology, there's a story about a mortal youth named Tithonus. Aurora, the goddess of dawn, fell in love with the boy and when Zeus, the king of the gods, promised to grant Aurora any gift she chose for her lover, she asked that Tithonus might live forever. But, in her haste she forgot to ask for eternal youth, so when Zeus granted her request, Tithonus was doomed to an eternity of perpetual aging as a grouchy old man… forever.

In the movie "Highlander," Angus McLeod was born in 1518 as an immortal being. He could not die and to me, the best part of the movie was the depiction of this immortal's agony here on earth as he watched everything he loved die forcing him to begin his life over and over again. He saw all of the ugliness, which man had caused over four centuries. He witnessed the Spanish Inquisition, Waterloo, the atrocities of the Third Reich, and more. He saw the slavery and bigotry of the eighteenth century, the slaughter of the Native American tribes after the Civil War. This man's life was a living Hell!

There is a very big difference between the ways our feeble minds picture eternal life versus God's idea of eternal life. Our understanding comes from Quantum Physics and is limited within the Time-Space Continuum.

Life is your spirit, but the soul of man has usurped the spirit's position and psychology is now forced to define "how" we live our lives based on the animating force of the soul instead of the spirit. As I said previously, the soul has usurped the spirit's place as our animating force. Let's discuss this now.

❖ **Body First Person** - When the body becomes our life, we live as animals.
❖ **Body-Mind In Sync** - When the soul becomes our life, we live as rebels and fugitives in a life of desires,

emotions, and will (consuming entities). This is the position of mankind today!

❖ **Mind First Person** - But when we come to live our life in the mind/spirit and by the spirit, though we still use our soul's faculties just as we do our physical faculties, they are now the servants of the spirit.

If you live as a consuming entity, you will always lose. In other words, to get, you must give - you must sacrifice! Have you ever wondered why you have so many anxieties, phobias, worries and fears? The reality of this world is evil. So what is reality? I will tell you. This is reality:

"Life without war is impossible either in nature or in grace. The basis of physical, mental, moral and spiritual life is antagonism. Health is the balance between physical life and external nature, and it is maintained only by sufficient vitality on the inside against things on the outside. Everything outside my physical life is designed to put me to death. Things, which keep me going when I am alive, disintegrate me when I am dead. If I have enough fighting power, I produce the balance of health.

The same is true of mental life. If I want to maintain a vigorous mental life, I have to fight, and in that way the mental balance called thought is produced. Morally it is the same. Everything that does not partake of the nature of virtue is the enemy of virtue in me, and it depends on what moral caliber I have whether I overcome and produce virtue (GOOD CHARACTER). Immediately I fight, I am moral in that particular. No man is virtuous because he cannot help it; virtue (character) is acquired.

- ❖ Psychology only studies the observable aspects of the mind and discounts the unseen or intangible aspects of the human mind.
- ❖ Behavioral science attempts to study the intangible aspects of the human mind…why you do the things you do and more importantly why you don't do what you should do.
- ❖ There is no such thing as commercial psychology versus personal psychology. The mind uses the same mechanism to evaluate all types of relationships.
- ❖ Everything we do revolves around relationships. We relate to our environment, our friends, family, co-workers, other people and even our pets. We are social animals.

The Mechanism of the Human Mind

Belief Systems + Thought + Delight = Action/Behavior/Conduct

Conscious Mind

5-senses:
Sight
Hearing
Taste
Touch
Smell
ESP (women only)

Subconscious Mind

Intellect:
Experiential
Empirical

DEW:
Desires, Emotions and Will

The Human Psyche Differences Between Genders

The female psyche operates on emotional, spiritual, physical and intellectual planes
The male psyche operates only on the intellectual and physical planes.

Here is an exercise you might find weird but it demonstrates the power of the human mind.

Fi yuo cna raed tihs, yuo hvae a sgtrane mnid too. Cna yuo raed tihs? Olny 55 plepoe out of 100 can. I cdnuolt blveiee taht I cluod aulaclty uesdnatnrd waht I was rdanieg. The phaonmneal pweor of the hmuan mnid, aoccdrnig to a rscheearch at Cmabrigde Uinervtisy, it dseno't mtaetr in waht oerdr the ltteres in a wrod are, the olny iproamtnt tihng is taht the frsit and lsat ltteer be in the rghit pclae. The rset can be a taotl mses and you can sitll raed it whotuit a pboerlm. Tihs is bcuseae the huamn mnid deos not raed ervey lteter by istlef, but the wrod as a wlohe. Azanmig huh? Yaeh and I awlyas tghuhot slpeling was ipmorantt!

You might have found it somewhat unusual that you could probably read the jumbled mess above. Actually over half the people that see this exercise can decipher the words at the same speed of reading as if the words were not jumbled.

It is important to note that the human mind thinks in packages…concepts rather than individual ideas.

Your eyes see each letter but the mind looks at the whole word instead. As you read, the mind looks at the first and last letter only. Remember this; the mind sees the beginning and end. We will talk about this later…

If you were to listen to an orchestra, your ear listens to every note from every instrument but a trained ear can actually pick out individual instruments from the whole sound as the mind hears the whole symphony.

How does this apply to you?

Learning to observe means going beyond the mind's natural ability to only read the first and last letters of a word!

It is training the mind to see all the letters, not just the eye but the mind!

Truisms About the Human Mind

❖ Pain vs. Pleasure – people are more motivated to avoid pain than seek pleasure.
❖ A person that is suffering depression will seek relief (notice I didn't say cure) before they seek happiness.

16

- ❖ The human mind cannot tell the difference between fantasy and reality.
- ❖ The human mind gravitates to the desires, emotions and will of its psyche. People crave entertainment so fantasy dominates their existences.
- ❖ The human mind is easily distracted! You can either be the cause of these distractions or other stimuli will be the cause but rest assured people WILL BE distracted because the human mind is gullible.

The human mind responds quickly to these three forms of stimuli

- ❖ Sex
- ❖ Humor
- ❖ FEAR

But the greatest of them all is FEAR!

BTW – on the positive side we have faith, hope, love, but the greatest of these *is* LOVE.

Fear usually takes the form of what is called "Scarcity Thought"

You are afraid that someone will have what you feel belongs to you or that others will have more "stuff" than you.

- ❖ The subconscious mind is often referred to as the "heart," and is the control mechanism the body uses to store our beliefs.

❖ **These beliefs are stored as pictures in our "hearts" and create frequencies in our bodies.**

❖ We know that the optimum human frequency is a little below 7.83 hertz. To drop below this frequency brings on the onslaught of disease. To rise above it a person demonstrates psychic abilities.

❖ Harmful beliefs that cause unhealthy frequencies are the source of almost all problems - physical, mental, emotional.

❖ The subconscious mind creates a belief system, which we call "pictures of the heart."

❖ These pictures involve either visions, or dreams/fantasies.

❖ Science has discovered that the subconscious mind cannot distinguish between fantasy and reality.

*The subject of all dreams is the dreamer.
*Dreams are born in our desires, emotions and will.
*Dreamers believe in a belief system, which is fantasy.
*A life lived within a fantasy creates a feeling of self-centeredness, hopelessness and despair. In dreams everything is perfect.
*The subject of a vision is not the visionary but the world.
*Visions are born in the intellect.
*Visions are pictures of the future that have already been experienced in the heart of those who give it birth.

18

*Visionaries sacrifice themselves for the good of mankind.
*Visions have a moral quality that transcends the self-centered nature of dreams.
*By its very nature a vision launches a mission, a "cause-that-inspires."
*Visions create a sense of belonging.

❖ We act upon visions and/or dreams, using thought.
❖ Thought employs the intellect, in the case of visions, or the desires, emotions and the will, in the case of dreams.
❖ Intellectual thought relies on wisdom; emotional thought relies on the pursuit of pleasure, comfort and delight.
❖ Dreamers live within a facade; they create a false sense of worth using imaginary situations.
❖ Visionaries live within reality; they create change, within a framework of restraint, and intellectual thought.
❖ The world is made up of OPPOSITES, which is usually the corrupted version of the original. We have good and evil. We have love and lust!
❖ EVERYTHING YOU DO IS BECAUSE OF LOVE OR LUST. Learn to love because there are no crimes beyond forgiveness.

*Love is born in the intellect; lust is born in the DEW!
*Love is vision; lust is fantasy.
*Love restrains & sacrifices; lust is selfish
*Love is being one with someone or something
*Lust is being with someone or something.
*Visionaries love; dreamers lust!

*Visionaries do what is required; dreamers just do their best!

WHEN THERE IS NO HOPE OF LOVE DO WE ABANDON OURSELVES TO LUST?

Yes we do!

Pictures of the heart are your belief system.

❖ We animate these pictures into either fantasies, or visions.
❖ People do not appear to see the difference between the matter part of an organism and the life part, which animates it.
❖ We seem to think that the organism itself is life. In other words, it is not our outward appearance that is our life, but our inward existence.
❖ Life is what goes into the body. Death is what comes out.
❖ A person who lies is not a liar because he tells a lie. The lie is the manifested behavior of some subconscious belief system. The lie only demonstrates that the person is a liar…it is the effect.
❖ Except for love, the power of words inspired by a vision or fantasy is the most potent human force.

"Do you want to have or do you want to be?"

*For a dreamer: "Seeing is believing!"
*But they only see imaginary things that are not real!!
*This is why "The Secret" is WRONG!
*Say it and claim it is WRONG!

*Blab it and grab it IS WRONG!
*See it and be it IS WRONG!
Dreamers practice companionship – To be with someone or something!

VERY IMPORTANT:

1. Dreamers covet the object of their temptation, BUT they covet <u>the temptation</u> more so than <u>the object</u> itself because <u>the temptation is the idol of their fantasy</u>.
2. If there is a conflict between the conscious and subconscious mind, the subconscious mind always wins…ALWAYS!
3. All reaction occurs in the conscious mind; all interaction occurs in the subconscious mind. Fear is a "REACTION" to losing control.

For a visionary: "Believing is seeing!"

There are no SECRETS; there are only challenges to be conquered!

THIS IS NOT A SECRET: Putting a photo of a Ferrari on your refrigerator and seeing yourself driving it by employing the so-called law of attraction is pure BUPKES!!! Why? Because this is all occurring in the conscious mind and beliefs reside in the subconscious mind. How do you transfer something from the conscious mind to the subconscious mind and make it a belief system?

A Ferrari is the object of your temptation but what you covet most is the temptation of owning a Ferrari because the temptation is the idol of your fantasy.

It is all about ATTENTION & ACCEPTANCE!!!!! I have a $100 bill in my hand and I am willing to give it to you. But if you don't ACCEPT it then it is still in my hand. BELIEF SYSTEMS ARE CREATED BY ATTENTION & ACCEPTANCE!

John 1:12 But as many as received him, to them gave he **the right** to become children of God, *even* to them that believe on his name

Human things must be known to be loved; but divine things must be loved to be known.

BELIEVING IS SEEING!

Let's talk about goals...which of the following goals are good goals?

❖ To want to get married and have a wonderful, happy, loving marriage?
❖ To want to have children who are happy, successful, and loving?
❖ To have a successful, fulfilling and rewarding career?
❖ Is it a good goal to want to have fun, bonded, loving, and meaningful relationships with other people?

Which of the listed goals are good goals? None of them!

You should never have anything for a goal that is not 100% under your control, AND each and every goal should be <u>motivated by love</u>.

Almost all goals that we have in our life are wrong.

Everything that we do, we do because of a goal we have.

When we get up in the morning, it's because of some goal that we have; we are hungry for breakfast, or we need to go to work.

If we go to the grocery store, it's because of some goal we have. If we are kind to people, it's because of some goal that we have.

Now we don't always know what they are, because a lot of these are subconscious goals.

The goals we have are the reasons for everything we do. But, do all of your goals involve only YOU?

Of course not!

And when the other person, or persons, in your goal do not perform, or act the way you want them to, then we become anxious and stressed.

When our goals get blocked, it creates anger, anxiety, and frustration. If we only have good goals, we will not experience anger or anxiety.

That's how you know, if you are living a wrongful goal. If the result is anger and frustration because your control was blocked and blocking your goal, then you had a wrongful goal. It may have been a fine and noble desire, but a wrongful goal.

Filters

We live in a society of consumerism and entertainment. In my previous books I have spoken reams about this subject. Instant gratification is paramount and today's technology delivers information and other stimuli in bucketfuls to the human mind. We have already spoken about filters that the human mind employs to weed out what it determines to be irrelevant. This "irrelevancy" is different in every individual and many times is programmed into our minds subconsciously or without us knowing it. We have also spoken about the causes of these various filters such as environment, maturity, upbringing, culture, etc.

The one essential common element of all filters is that they are all ATTENTION diverters. We have spoken about attention earlier; what is very interesting is that filters are generally viewed as bad when some are really very good.

I had a friend, who lives in Chicago, fall on hard times and needed assistance. When I got to him he was living in a cheap hotel and had a room so small when you put the key in the door you broke the *window (I slay me)*. His room was about 50 feet from the Loop (the overhead train that circles around Chicago). The noise was deafening when the train went by, and it went by often, but my friend had filtered it out. Amazing, but when you thing about it, my friend really does hear the train but yet he

24

pays no attention to it, so in actuality, it is like he doesn't hear it at all! So filters divert attention, and take away our focus; so let's talk about focus.

The Incredible Power of Focus

One of the more important points I have made has been the idea that you really do create your own life and your own reality. I know this idea has become a kind of personal growth cliché that many of us have heard over and over for years. Many people, after continuing to experience the same old ups and downs and personal dramas over many years, get to the point where they dismiss this idea as charming but useless -- or just plain wrong. "If I'm creating this, then I'm certainly not doing it on purpose," they say. "It sure seems like this is HAPPENING to me, rather than that I'm creating it." They just assume that it's all BS because "this and this and this and this are going on for me, and I have no control over it, and anyone who thinks I'm creating this doesn't understand what I'm going through." Essentially, they are resigning themselves to becoming a victim of circumstances.

We live in a universe of infinite complexity and many forces -- way too many to keep track of -- operate on us. Yes, it is true that we are NOT in control of everything that happens, because we are not in control of most of those infinite other parts of the universe. In fact, the only thing you have total and complete control over is...YOUR OWN MIND. That is, if you learn how to exercise it.

Luckily, this one thing -- your mind -- that you do have control over gives you tremendous power. By exercising control over your mind, you can get the rest of those infinite other parts of the universe to begin to march in formation.

The person who says, "If I'm creating this, it certainly isn't on purpose," is right. They are not creating what is happening to them "on purpose." Who would purposely create failure, or bad relationships, or any other kind of suffering? You can only do something that is not good for you that is harmful to you, if you do it subconsciously. This means if you are creating something you don't want, you must be doing so subconsciously.

Your mind is running on automatic pilot, based on "software" (subconscious programming) installed when you were too young to know any better, by parents, teachers, friends, the media, and other experiences and influences. The key is to become more conscious, more aware...to get yourself off automatic pilot. Once you do this, you stop creating all the dramas and other garbage you don't want in your life.

How do you do this? One way is by remembering and using a very important piece of wisdom. What is this important piece of wisdom? I'm glad you asked.

It's the fact that whatever you focus on manifests as reality in your life.

You are always focusing on something, whether you are aware of it or not. If I spent some time with you, and heard your history, I could tell you what you are focusing on. How? By looking at the results you are getting in your life. The results you get are always the result of your focus.

The problem is this focus is usually not conscious focus; it's automatic or subconscious focus. We subconsciously focus on something we don't want, and then when we get it we feel like a victim and don't even stop to think that we created it in the first place. And what is more, we don't realize we could choose to create something completely different if we could only get out of the cycle of subconsciously focusing on something other than what we want.

If you have a significant negative emotional experience (say, for instance, a relationship in which you are abused or mistreated in some way), a part of you is going to say: "Okay, I get it. There are people out there who can and will hurt me. Relationships can be dangerous and painful. I have to watch out for these people [or sometimes, relationships in general] and avoid them." Unfortunately, to watch out for them and avoid them, you have to focus your mind on "people who could hurt me," or "bad relationships," and that focus draws more of what you don't want to you...AND...actually makes these things you don't want (at least initially) attractive to you, so when they appear in your life you are drawn to them. This is why many people keep having one relationship after another with the same person, but in different bodies. This, of course, applies to everything, not just relationships. I'm just using relationships as an example.

Focusing on what you do not want, ironically, makes it happen. Focusing on not being poor makes you poor. Focusing on not making mistakes causes you to make mistakes. Focusing on not having a bad relationship creates bad relationships. Focusing on not being depressed makes you depressed. Focusing on not smoking makes you want to smoke. And so on. I think you get the idea. The mind will create what you focus on both GOOD and BAD!!!

27

The truth is your mind cannot tell the difference between something you think about or focus on that you DO want, and something you think about or focus on but do NOT want. The mind is a goal-seeking mechanism, and an extremely effective one at that. Already, all the time, it is elegantly and precisely creating exactly what you focus on. You are already a World Champion Expert at creating whatever you focus on. You couldn't get any better at it, and you don't need to get any better at it.

When you focus on anything, your mind says: "Okay, we can do that," and starts figuring out how to do it. It doesn't ask whether you're focusing on it because you want it or because you do not want it. It ALWAYS assumes you want what you focus on and then it goes and makes it happen. The more frequent and the more intense the focus, the faster and more completely you will create what you have focused on, which is why intense negative experiences create intense focus on what you do not want, and tend to make you re-create what you don't want, over and over.

Most of the time, for most people, all the focusing and thinking is going by at warp speed, on automatic, without much, if any, conscious intention. Your job is to learn how to direct this power by consciously directing your focus to the outcomes you want. Once you do, everything changes. This does, however, take some work, because at first you have to swim upstream against the current of your old, unconscious habits, and the current can be swift and strong. Trained observation actually teaches you to focus on what you want.

First, you have to discover all the things you focus on that you do not want, and I'm willing to bet there are quite a few -- way more than you think. To the degree you're getting what you don't want, you are focusing, albeit subconsciously, on what you don't want.

Spend some time over the next few weeks making a list of all the things you do NOT want as you notice yourself thinking about them.

Second, you have to get very clear about what you DO want. Then, you have to examine each of the things you want and be sure they are not just something you do NOT want in disguise. For instance, saying "I want a relationship where I am treated well" would not even be an issue if you had not had relationships where you were not treated well, and even in making this seemingly positive statement you are focusing on not wanting to be mistreated. Saying "I want a reliable car" wouldn't even come up if you weren't focusing on the fact that you don't want a car that breaks down and needs a lot of repairs.

After you've sorted out the things you habitually focus on that you do not want, and know what you do want, you have to begin to notice each time you think about an outcome you do not want, and consciously change your thinking, right in that moment, so you are instead focusing on what you do want.

Remember, you do NOT have to avoid things to be happy and get what you want. The urge to avoid something is a result of having had a negative emotional experience regarding that thing, and trying to avoid things requires you to focus on them, which tells your brain to create them. Not good.

You will be surprised how often you are thinking about what you do not want, how difficult it is to catch yourself

29

doing it every time, and -- most of all – how difficult it is to switch your thinking to what you DO want. There is a strong momentum to keep thinking about that thing you want to avoid. As I said, the current is strong and swift, especially at first.

The solution? Practice, practice, practice. Persistence, persistence, persistence!!!

It's a very good idea to write down what you want, very specifically, so that your Fairy Godmother, were she to read it, would know exactly what to give you without any additional explanation.

Then, read what you have written to yourself, preferably out loud, several times a day, while seeing yourself, in your mind, already having what you want.

Believing is seeing and not the other way around as the world teaches you!

The more emotion you can bring to it, the better. Then, take whatever action is available to begin moving toward what you want. A good time to do this reading and visualizing is when you first wake up and before you go to bed.

I know this is work. Do it anyway. There is a price for everything, and this is the price you must pay to get what you want. Be prepared to pay it. It will be worth it, I promise. And be prepared to pay for a while before you get results. Stick with it.

Another way to change your focus is to ask questions. As an example, I'll ask you one right now. What did you have for breakfast this morning? To answer this question (even to just internally process the question), you had to shift your focus from whatever your mind was focused on (hopefully, to what I am teaching) to today's breakfast.

This means that to change your focus, all you have to do is...ask yourself a question!

It also means you better be careful what questions you ask yourself. Good questions include "How can I get X?" "How can I do X?" "How can I be X?" By asking these kinds of questions, you get your mind to focus on what you want to have, do, or be. Then, your mind takes over and answers the question...solves the problem...and creates what you want. You just have to provide the focus, take whatever action presents itself, and be persistent (some things take time).

I would do away with questions like "What's wrong with me?" or "Why can't I find someone to love me?" and so on. Your mind will find an answer to any question you give it, including these disempowering questions.

Learn to say "How can I...?" when you don't know what to do, instead of "I can't," and (if you are persistent in asking) you will receive the answer, every time. Learn to be conscious in what you focus on and your whole life will change.

This all may seem very utopian to you, or overly simplistic, or like a lot of work. I assure you it is not utopian (it's the way all successful people think), it IS simple, but not simplistic, and yes, it is work, at first. The great Napoleon Hill, who spent over 60 years studying the most effective and most successful people of the 20th century, concluded that -- without exception -- "whatever the mind can conceive and believe, it can achieve." He at first suspected there had to be exceptions, but toward the

31

end of his life he said he had to admit he had not found ANY.

Let's go over that again: "Whatever the mind can conceive and believe it can achieve."

It will take some time to learn how to consciously focus your mind. It will require some effort. You will fail many times, and it will seem difficult. But at a certain point you will "get it" and at that point it will become as automatic as the unconscious focusing you have been doing. When that happens, a whole new universe of power will open to you.

More on Focusing

"And be not conformed to this age, but be transformed by the renewing of your mind, in order to prove by you what is the good and pleasing and perfect will of God."

The one thing in your life you can command is your own mind. Whatever negative people and situations you face, you can always choose a positive attitude. But doing so requires a firm, strong commitment.

Helpful: Begin by writing a self-convincing creed – I believe I can direct and control my emotions, intellect and habits with the intention of developing a positive mental attitude. Post it where you'll see it when you get up in the morning. Read it during the day, and say it aloud. Speaking an intention reinforces it. Choose a "self-motivator" – a meaningful phrase tailored to help you reach your positive thinking goals. Examples:

> • Counter discouragement with the phrase "Every problem contains the seed of its own solution."

- Fight procrastination with "Do it now."

Keep your self-motivators nearby – in your pocket or on your desk – and repeat them throughout the day to instill these important new values.

Develop A Life Plan. Setting short and long-term goals each day creates a road map for your life. But only set GOOD goals!!! What is a good goal? One where you are 100% in control and one that is founded in love! A goal of raising good, healthy and prosperous children is a bad goal because you are not in control of what your kids choose. See the important difference? The goal is noble but it is not a good goal.

You identify where you're going, focus your mind on getting there and avoid many wrong turns.

Helpful: Use the D-E-S-I-R-E formula as a goal-setting guideline...

- **D**etermine what you want. Be exact, and express the goal positively. Say what you want to be or do rather than what you don't want.

- **E**valuate what you'll give in return. How much work will you do to turn your plan into action?

- **S**et a date for your goal. Be realistic, allowing enough time without postponing it too long.

- **I**dentify a step by step plan. Devise immediate, small steps to get started.

- **R**epeat your plan in writing.

- **E**ach and every day, morning and evening, read your plan aloud as you picture yourself already having achieved your goals.

Writing out your daily goals helps maintain your motivation. Keep them in your pocket or purse to read frequently throughout the day.

The Power of Visualization
Because visual images reach into our deepest mental levels, I have found pictures to be profound motivational tools. Why? Remember the mind holds everything as pictures!

Helpful: Make a list of personal qualities you want to develop...write down the names of people with whom you would like to have better relationships. Now clip pictures from magazines and newspapers that symbolize your goals.

Example: If generosity is your chosen quality, you could use a photo of someone with an outstretched hand.

Put the pictures where you'll see them everyday...and believe that you will get what you have visualized. You may also create your own "mental pictures" to defeat negative thoughts, such as dwelling on past reversals. Maintain A Positive Focus. Giving yourself positive experiences actually reinforces your positive attitude. Examples...

- Treat your five senses every day. Listen to your favorite music, taste a food you love, enjoy a beautiful view, etc.

- Cultivate a sense of humor. Laughter relaxes tension, and seeing the funny side of things helps you take yourself less seriously.

- Smile when you feel like frowning. Smile at yourself in the mirror. If this makes you laugh at yourself, the smile will be that much more real.

Now realize the optimistic face you show the world creates positive thoughts about you in everyone you meet.

How to Train Your Subconscious Mind

Did you know that often the difference between success and failure is the ability to train your mind to focus on achieving your goals and not focus on problems? It's been proven by researchers and by some of the most successful people in the world.

Getting your mind to focus and concentrate on success - so that it finds solutions instead of focusing on the problems is usually the difference between success and failure. But how do you do this?

I'm about to show you how. I'll outline the importance of training your mind, how to start directing your subconscious mind, and how to keep your mind focused so that you constantly achieve your goals and live the life you want. Disciplining your mind so that it is focused on your goals is crucial to your success. If your mind is not trained to focus on and achieve your goals then you really have little chance of success. Your conscious mind is a direct link to your subconscious mind.

So if your mind is focused on your goals and is trained to achieve those goals then your subconscious mind will also be focused on those goals and will attract the situations and opportunities for you to achieve the success you want. It's really that simple.

The minute you get distracted for a prolonged period - you lose sight of your objective and fail to accomplish those goals. In order for to enjoy success - the mind has to be regularly focused on your goals - you can't stay focused for short bursts and expect to get results.

Think of it this way, your riding in a car driven by your personal driver and every time your driver asks you where you want to go you simply say: "I don't know. Wherever you want to go is fine with me." Then when your driver takes you to the place of his choice you complain and say: "I don't want to be here, take me somewhere else." And again you say you don't know where you want to go.

Can you see the confusion you would create? Can you see how you would never get to where you want to go because you haven't trained your driver to automatically take you where you want to go? You haven't given him the proper instructions.

Your mind and subconscious mind work the same way. If you don't train your mind to focus on your goals then your subconscious mind cannot create the situations that will help you achieve those goals. When you keep changing your mind, when you are not clear on what you want - your subconscious gets confused - and you end up exactly where you don't want to be.

Let's go back to the example of your personal driver. Wouldn't it be a lot easier and more comfortable if you told your driver where you wanted to go - or even better - your driver knew where you wanted to go ahead of time? But that will only happen when you train your driver by repeatedly telling him where you want to go on a regular basis.

Your subconscious mind is your driver. Your subconscious gets its instructions from your thoughts and beliefs. Give your subconscious the right instructions and it will take you where ever you want to go in life. When your mind is focused on your goals you direct your subconscious to create opportunities for you to achieve your goals. Your responsibility is to follow up on these opportunities.

How You Can Train Your Mind

Believe it or not I get a lot of calls and emails everyday from people who want to achieve their goals but simply can't get their mind to focus on the tasks that need to be done to have the success that they want. This happens because the mind is simply not used to focusing on your goals and following up with completing those tasks. So how do you get your mind to change? How do you train your mind?

The first step is to get the mind to stop doing what it is used to doing - or break the pattern that you've been following for so long. This will require some effort - but the reward will allow you to live the life you want and enjoy the level of success that you want.

To re-train your mind and direct your subconscious mind you start by paying more attention - so that when you see yourself getting distracted and not following up on things that you wanted to do - you take a step to break the pattern. You can break the pattern by doing something else. For example: you can start following up on what you had planned to do, you can create a list and follow up with it regularly to see if you are on track.

One thing that always works is to think about your goals every morning. As you're in bed, think about your goals and think about what you can do to achieve them during the day. If you find that you constantly say: "I don't know what do to do to achieve my goals." Then you're not looking for answers in the right place.

Take a look at what other people have done to achieve similar goals and see if you can follow the same process. For example: If you want to make more money take a look at someone else who has made a lot of money and see what they've done. Can you follow their process? Maybe you can even talk to them about the process? If you want to meet someone and be in a healthy relationship, talk to a friend who is in a successful relationship and find out what they did. By doing the above exercises you train your mind to focus on finding solutions while at the same time you direct your subconscious mind to create the opportunities for you to succeed. And - you begin to create a new pattern of thinking and you start to train the mind to work differently. You're now telling your driver where you want to go. This eliminates the confusion and allows you to achieve your goals.

You're not going to magically get your mind to focus or concentrate without you taking some form of action. When you finally do take some action your mind will still resist - but as you continue taking action the resistance will subside - REPITITION. So what action can you take? First start with the exercise I just outlined above. Next - meditate. Meditation is one of the best ways to relax and calm your mind while training it to focus on what you want. When you meditate you actually start to clear the clutter that dominates your mind.

Make the Time

Finally it seems a lot of people have come to believe that they just don't have the time to achieve their goals. If you are one of the many who have such a belief then you've really convinced yourself that your goals are not worthy of your time; because if they were you would make the time for them. I'm not talking about spending an entire day or even a few hours. It's only a few minutes at different intervals. Why try to get everything crammed into one hour? Why not try to think about your goals at different intervals during the day? For example: you may have a few minutes while you're taking a walk - think of your achieving your goals. You could also do this while you're taking a shower, driving, walking, anytime. Here's a suggestion; the next time you are driving or taking a shower, pay attention to your thoughts. Are these thoughts actually working for your or against you? Would it be better to focus on your goals or keep recycling the negative clutter or junk in your head? The choice is yours - and taking action is really about taking a small step. You don't need to spend hours meditating. Even if you simply mediated for 5 or 10 minutes a day you'd be able to increase your ability to concentrate and focus by a 100-percent within a matter of days! Do it for weeks or months and you'll have dramatic results!

How to Put Your Mind to Sleep Quickly and Rest Completely

If you often lay awake, unable to put your mind to rest while you're tossing and turning, you're going to love what you're about to read, because I'm about to share with you one of the most powerful methods for quickly shutting off your mind, and drifting off to sleep.

As you may already know, your mind must be in the Alpha brain-wave stage to fall asleep. This is the stage your mind enters you're still conscious, but your body and begin to relax. It enables your more rampant and conscious mind to turn off as you enter the realm of sleep. We all know how it feels... when you're lying awake in bed trying to fall asleep, it seems like your mind is running on hyper-speed. It's almost like you're thinking 10 times faster than when you're just normally awake and alert. In fact, if you experience this often, I can tell you for a fact that your mind IS working harder than it is when you're not trying to fall asleep, and there is a very good reason for it, here's why this happens. In my books and articles on sleep, I often teach a principle: "What you focus on expands." You see, your mind responds to focus, and it goes hand in hand with the law of momentum. What is the law of momentum? Quite simply:

"Energy in motion, tends to STAY in motion"

"Energy stopped, tends to STAY stopped"

In other words, if you take action in your life, and begin to create success, you will experience more and more success every day. Success breeds success. On the other hand, if you sit your butt down on the couch to watch TV and say, "Aww, just one show, I'll only watch one show," very soon you'll be sitting there for four hours, and you'll watch five or six shows.

The law of momentum is everywhere in life, in physics, with your body, and most importantly, with your "thoughts." You see, your thinking is very predictable; it all works on the law of focus and momentum. Your mind is like a big ball of potential thinking energy, just waiting for you to give it a direction to think wildly into. It awaits and responds your every command. It's an exceptional tool except, most of us aren't very experienced at "controlling" this amazing tool. In fact, a lot people aren't even aware that they can control it! And this is where sleep problems come in.

Imagine your mind like a giant overflowing lake that's just waiting for an outlet to pour into... Slowly, when it finds an outlet, it begins with a trickle of water. That trickle turns into a stream. Then, that stream turns into a small river. Pretty soon, the small river is a giant unstoppable waterfall. Your thoughts work in the same way when you're "trying" to fall asleep.

For example, you're lying in bed, frustrated, forcing your mind to not think. "I just want to get some sleep! Stop thinking! Okay, starting now... I won't think anymore. No think... nothing. My life is nothing... If only I would finally get motivated in my job maybe I would finally create the income to start traveling instead of dealing with these problems. Problems, how can I... Ahh, I'm thinking again! Stop it!"

You get even more frustrated, and repeat the process over again in a few minutes. So how do you stop it? It's easy, you see, you can easily control your thinking, except most people aren't aware of the tools necessary! The good news is, I'm about to give you the 3-step handbook to controlling your mind. Here are the 3-universal steps that will enable you to not only stop thinking; you'll also be able to lower your brain-waves into the alpha brain-state, which will quickly let you enter sleep...

Awareness
The first step to changing anything is becoming aware that it's happening, especially if it's your mind. Pretend your mind is racing, and you finally realize that you're

41

thinking... Most people at this stage get extremely frustrated and "try" to force the mind into submission. It doesn't work! Why? Because, what you focus on expands. The more frustrated you get, the more you're focusing on frustration, so you'll get even MORE frustration and more thinking... on and on!

So the first step is to simply become "aware" of the fact that you're thinking. Nothing more. When you notice that you're thinking, smile to yourself, and say, "I just noticed myself thinking... Interesting..." Now notice what happens inside of you when you do this... something VERY profound. If "I" just noticed "myself" thinking, perhaps there are really two completely separate identities running your life? There is the "I" and there is the "self."

The "I", is the real you, the higher being, the "I" behind the mind, that runs the show, the heart, the soul, the true conscious being, the choice maker.

The "self" is the mind; if left to run the show, it will run in endless circles until the edge of insanity.

The moment you do this, the moment you become "aware" - you are no longer a slave to your mind. You have won. After you become aware... do nothing, just lay there for 3 seconds and notice how it feels to be present in who you really are, not the mind, but you, the "I" - there is a great feeling of peace behind that presence in the "I." Why? Because when you are aware like this, you're aware of the power of your choice making. You now have the power of choice.

Relaxed Focus

"What you focus on expands." Now that you have become aware of your thinking, all you have to do is "direct" your mind into a place that will bring you into a deep, deep place of relaxation. Think about it, if before your mind will relentlessly race into any direction you give it; why not pick a direction that will give you peace and restful sleep?

But, most people don't know what that direction really is. It's really easy. If you focus on anything your body does or feels subconsciously, you will begin to become more and more realized. For example your breathing, the feeling of the pillow on your head, the sounds of nature outside (unless you live in the city), the warmth of your body. These are all things that happen, yet your conscious mind doesn't think about them.

As you know, "What you focus on expands"... So what would happen if you focused on something that is happening in your "subconscious"? That's right, your conscious thinking would diminish, and your subconscious mind would begin to take over the entire process of you falling asleep! It really is that simple, and it works every-time.

The easiest one is your breathing. And I promise you if you just try this tonight, you will be shocked when you wake up in the morning: "Wow! It worked!"

Repetition
As I said, the easiest one to focus on is your breathing. In the beginning, you'll find this easier said than done. Let me walk you through it.

43

- Begin by taking your focus onto your breathing. Take a deep breath in. Hold it for a short while, and slowly exhale...

- Count "1"

- Breathe in again... hold it shortly, exhale slowly, and count...

- "2"

Why count? Because I guarantee you, in the very beginning, you may find it challenging to hold your focus. In fact, you'll be surprised as you may not even make it to "5" the first time. This is because your conscious ever-thinking mind will butt in and interrupt. You may randomly go off into a barrage of thoughts again. If this happens, and it very well may, what do you do?

Simply become aware, and begin focusing on your breathing again. Guess what happens? As you become aware, 2 or 3 times... your mind will give up. I guarantee you, beyond the shadow of a doubt, when you get to "10" or "15" breaths you will feel a wave of relaxation in your body. This is the silent "click" as your mind shifts from the high frequency Beta brain-waves into Alpha brain-waves. Your subconscious mind will do the rest!

Chapter 1 – Cyber Webs of Deception, Lies and Manipulation

Cybercrime is made up of numerous individuals but the really bad and pervasive cybercrime is conducted by ten notorious cyber-gangs...

The Problem is Organized

Most cyber-crime is conducted by 10-worldwide gangs.

The 10-Most Notorious Cyber Gangs

1-Russian Business Network
2-Rock Phish Gang
3-NSA
4-Grey Pigeon Authors
5-Stormworm Gang
6-Awola Crew
7-DRG Group
8-South American Groups
9-Oga-Nigerian
10-Individual Hackers (Anonymous)

As cyber-crime increases, so does their income and this feeds the increase of more cyber-crime.

Like drugs, cyber-crime pays and it pays very well.

Corporate Espionage is the most cyber-criminal activity and at the same time, the least protected area of vulnerability. And it is not being conducted just by nation-states against USA businesses either. The Gang of 10 hacking organizations cost American businesses an estimated $2-billion every year.

The New York Times

False Tax Returns
With Personal Data in Hand, Thieves File Early and Often

MIAMI — Besieged by identity theft, Florida now faces a fast-spreading form of fraud so simple and lucrative that some violent criminals have traded their guns for laptops. And the target is the United States Treasury.

J. Russell George, the Treasury inspector general for tax administration, testified before Congress this month that the I.R.S. detected 940,000 fake returns for 2010 in which identity thieves would have received $6.5 billion in refunds. But Mr. George said the agency missed an additional 1.5 million returns with possibly fraudulent refunds worth more than $5.2 billion.

From 2008 to 2011, the number of returns filed by identity thieves and stopped by the I.R.S. increased significantly, officials said. Last year, it was at least 1.3 million, said Steven T. Miller, deputy commissioner for services and enforcement at the agency. This year, with only 30 percent of the filings reviewed so far, the number is already at 2.6 million. The bulk is related to identity theft, Mr. Miller said.

47

**Teen recounts horror of abduction into sex slavery
Many young victims of human traffickers treated as
criminals themselves**

For someone who's only 18, Shauna Newell is remarkably composed as she describes being kidnapped, drugged, gang-raped and savagely beaten. It is only when she talks about seeing one of the men who sexually assaulted her — free and unafraid of being prosecuted — that she starts to break down.

"I went out to the beach a few weeks ago and I saw the dude who raped me, and he just looked at me," Newell told NBC News, her voice choking. "Like, hey ... you ruined my whole life. You have scared me for the rest of my life and you're just sitting there going on with your life like nothing is wrong."

Child Abduction

FHP - *Mall* & Shopping Safety
www.flhsmv.gov/fhp/misc/christmas/mst.htm
More than 100000 *children* are *abducted* every year -- often in *malls* or department stores, according to the National Center for Missing and Exploited *Children...*

48

The day I was almost *abducted* & killed by a *child* predator - Kanuk...

*http://open.salon.com/blog/kanuk/2010/06/22/the_day_i_*
was_almost_abducted_killed_by_a_child_predator
Jun 22, 2010 – The day I was almost *abducted* & killed by a *child* predator ... So I went on my way and walked to the *mall's* record store. Remember those?

Is a fifth grader old enough to go to the *mall* by himself?

http://www.wiki.answers.com
And don't forget that even adult women have been *kidnapped from malls*, as well as other public places, so why would you think your *child* would be an exception...

SulphurDailyNews.com

Dreamboard

This week, the United States Attorney joined forces with the Attorney General and Department of Homeland Security to announce the largest United States prosecution of an international criminal network.

What's even worse about this particular case ... **the criminal organization was developed to sexually exploit children.**

Dating back to December of 2009, the investigation targeted 72 defendants and more than 500 individuals around the world for their participation in an online

49

organization called, **"Dreamboard." This private, members-only online bulletin board was created and operated to promote pedophilia and encourage the sexual abuse of very young children.**

If you have young children, you may want to pay close attention to the particulars of this case. Let us warn you, however, it's not pleasant, but it is reality.

It gets worse...

ℭ𝔥𝔢 𝔇𝔞𝔦𝔩𝔶 𝔇𝔬𝔱

¡Viva Anonymous! The hacker gang is back in Mexico

"I strongly doubt the kidnapping took place," said the chief forensics investigator for ForensicsNation, which tracks hackers and groups like Anonuymous. "The cartel are not afraid of Anonymous."

THE WALL STREET JOURNAL

'Stingray' Phone Tracker Fuels Constitutional Clash

The New York Times

Justices Say GPS Tracker Violated Privacy Rights

abc NEWS

LulzSec 'Leader' Turns on Fellow Hacktivists:Feds

The Washington Post

The Feds concerned about hackers opening Prison doors

The New York Times

In Attack on Vatican Web Site, a Glimpse of Hackers' Tactics

YAHOO! NEWS

Minnesota Wi-Fi hacker gets 18 years in prison for terrorizing neighbors

theguardian

Feds versus the hacker underground: army of informers turned by fear

Mail Online

And then you have what is being called "Not-So Legal Hacking of your personal info
Sinister truth about Google spies: Street View cars stole information from British households but executives 'covered it up' for years. Work of Street View cars to be examined over allegations Google used them to download personal details - Emails, texts, photos and documents taken from Wi-Fi networks as cars photographed British roads. Engineer who designed software said a privacy lawyer should be consulted

amazon.com

Think different.

Even the government is spying on you...if you use certain words. Revealed: Hundreds of words to avoid using online if you don't want the government spying on you (and they include 'pork', 'cloud' and 'Mexico'). Department of Homeland Security forced to release list following freedom of information request. Agency insists it only looks for evidence of genuine threats to the U.S. and not for signs of general dissent. The words are included in the department's 2011 'Analyst's Desktop Binder' used by workers at their National Operations Center which instructs workers to identify 'media reports that reflect adversely on DHS and response activities'.

Cyber Criminals Are Organized

Hackers have their own news organization, their own news network. They even have their own education system and even their own movie. What's next? Locusts? Boils?

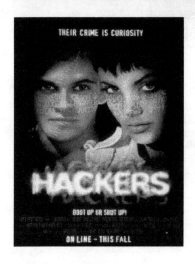

Actually the Hacker Underground is complete with their own news sites, news networks and these are really good things. These sites are where hackers BUY their information from other hackers. Info such as identity theft financial records, social security numbers, etc.

So, we pose as buyers or sellers and "bait" the hackers. When they respond we plant a tracking bug into their computer systems and instantly they go into our databases.

Now you may ask how do hackers pay for this information without revealing their identities? They use companies like Xoom.com...no questions asked, the hacker bank...but even their systems are not that secure (lol). They also use companies like Payza, because it is offshore and outside the regulations of The Patriot Act.

Hackers teach other hackers. Look...

CISPA means the "Cyber Intelligence Sharing and Protection Act"

How To Become A Hacker
Eric Steven Raymond

Table of Contents

#1 Target of Hackers and Crackers
LAW ENFORCEMENT

#2 Target of Hackers and Crackers - YOU!

Hackers and Crackers go after YOU in this order of importance

1. Children – predators are most active in child abduction and abuse.
2. Women – everything from stalking to voyeurism to sex slavery.
3. Businesses – small business are more often targeted due to less protective measures.
4. General Population – in the form of various cyber crimes such as identity theft, computer intrusion, and phishing scams.
5. Government Agencies – patient records on file with state record keepers getting hacked.

Areas of Personal EXPOSURE

- Credit Card Fraud
- Identity Theft
- Financial Scams
- Child Predation
- Computer Hijacking
- Malware, Spyware
- Electronic Voyeurism
- Viruses

- Keystroke Logging
- Phishing
- User Account & Password Theft
- Cell Phone Spying
- Online Auction Fraud – Ebay, etc.
- And much more…

The above areas of personal exposure are the more prevalent forms of cyber crimes directed against individuals. It is by no means a complete list.

The main problem is that the average computer user has no idea that they are exposed and even if they do, they have no idea how to protect themselves.

As technology expands, the tools available to the hacker and cyber-criminal expand too. They keep up with everything on the Internet where the average user does not.

Cyber-criminals are organizing into gangs. The most famous is the hacking gang called Anonymous that used "Denial of Service" techniques against major financial institutions that denied Wikileaks merchant account facilities in 2011.

But in countries such as Russia and many of the old "iron curtain" countries too, organized cyber-crime gangs are increasing.

The following Corporate Checklist is designed to identify the main and common areas of vulnerability.

Corporate Checklist

Part 1: The hacker subculture and approach
• An overview of the risks and threats
• An insight into the hacker underground
• The anatomy of a hack

Part 2: TCP/IP fundamentals
• TCP/IP and its relevance to hacking
• TCP header, flags and options
• UDP, ICMP and ARP
• Network traffic dump analysis
• Class exercises and lab sessions

Part 3: Reconnaissance techniques
• Selecting a target
• Identifying target hosts and services
• Network mapping techniques
• Fingerprinting and OS determination
• Scanning and stealth techniques
• Class exercises and lab sessions

Part 4: Compromising networks
• Vulnerability cross referencing
• Code auditing and insecure code examples
• Exploiting network services
• Sniffers, backdoors and root kits
• Trojans and session hijacking
• Denial of service attacks
• Trust exploitation and spoofing
• Buffer overflow techniques
• Web page graffiti attacks
• War dialers and dial-in hacking

• Manipulating audit trails and security logs
• Class exercises and lab sessions

Part 5: Windows Applied Hacking
• Windows components, Domains and structures
• Remote information gathering
• Scanning and banner checking
• Selecting services to attack
• Enumerating Windows information
• Windows hacking techniques
• Recent Windows vulnerabilities
• Class exercises and lab sessions

Part 6: Windows effective countermeasures
• User account policies and group allocations
• File and directory permissions
• File and print shares
• Hardening the registry
• Domains and trust relationships
• Securing network services
• Windows antivirus strategies
• Windows and Internet security
• Windows auditing and security logs
• Windows service packs and hot fixes
• Class exercises and lab sessions

Part 7: Unix applied hacking
• Unix components
• Unix variants
• Remote and local information gathering
• Scanning and fingerprinting
• Selecting services to attack
• Unix hacking techniques

• Recent Unix vulnerabilities
• Class exercises and lab sessions

Part 8: Unix effective countermeasures
• Unix password and group files
• User account and password controls
• Controlling command line access
• File and directory permissions
• SUID and SGID controls
• Crontab security
• Network and trust relationships
• Securing network services
• Unix antivirus strategies
• Unix and Internet security
• Unix auditing and security logs
• Unix security patches
• Class exercises and lab sessions

Part 9: Network security strategies
• Risk management and AS/NZS 4360
• Security management and AS/NZS 7799
• Developing a practical security strategy
• Physical security and environmental controls
• Personnel security and awareness training
• Firewall risks and strategies
• Intrusion detection system risks and strategies
• An overview of ecommerce security issues
• An overview of wireless security issues
• An overview of PBX security issues
• An overview of intrusion analysis techniques
• An overview of forensics procedures
• An overview of IT contingency planning
• Class exercises and lab sessions

Part 10: Advanced Security Techniques
*Inventory of Authorized and Unauthorized Devices
*Inventory of Authorized and Unauthorized Software
*Secure Configurations for Hardware and Software on Laptops, Workstations, and Servers
*Continuous Vulnerability Assessment and Remediation
*Malware Defenses
*Application Software Security
*Wireless Device Control
*Data Recovery Capability
*Security Skills Assessment and Appropriate Training to Fill Gaps
*Secure Configurations for Network Devices such as Firewalls, Routers, and Switches
*Limitation and Control of Network Ports, Protocols, and Services
*Controlled Use of Administrative Privileges
*Boundary Defense
*Maintenance, Monitoring, and Analysis of Security Audit Logs
*Controlled Access Based on the Need to Know
*Account Monitoring and Control
*Data Loss Prevention
*Incident Response Capability
*Secure Network Engineering
*Penetration Tests and Red Team Exercises

Prevention is the answer and by analyzing your vulnerabilities before cyber criminals strike, you can prevent some undeserved heartache and loss of assets.

Chapter 2 – Character is Acquired; Reputations Are Made

This is a subject that knocks people down most of the time and prevents their success from becoming reality. And this is where self-deception usually rears its ugly head.

Reputations are made while character is acquired and both are based on underlying belief systems. In Christianity it says that if a person takes care of his/her character, God will take care of the person's reputation but only if you live there in the Word of God. A famous writer viewed her faith not as a substitute for seeing, but as the light by which she saw really figured it out correctly. Most people view faith as believing in something you cannot see and this is not true. This is how the Judeo-Christian bible puts it:

Heb 11:1 Now faith is the assurance of things hoped for, the conviction of things not seen.

The definition of faith above emphasizes mental understanding as opposed to experiential knowledge or intuitive perception. In Chapter 1, I taught you that perception rules the human psyche rather than reality. Think about the perceptions you have and how they different from reality.

Thus, a life of genuine wisdom is a life founded upon the fear of the Lord and supported by genuine purity, peaceableness, gentleness, reasonableness, helpfulness, humility, and sincerity. Such a house will never fall! "Nearly all men die of their medicines, and not of their maladies." - French playwright Moliere

We have all known people who seem blind to their own malady, and people who would prefer their pain to change. Take this statement to the bank. In my experience as a doctor, patients are more interested in having me take away the pain rather than the cure. "Hey Doc, just give me a pill" is there battle cry. Really? Seriously? Don't you want to get better? No, they just want to feel better. Look around, drug addiction is everywhere. And drug addiction is nothing more than self-medicating yourself away from your suffering.

Are you obese? It is because you believe in being obese. How many of you have set a New Year's resolution to lose weight and have failed? It is because you don't believe in losing weight. Oh, you say you do but this is a conscious mind belief and nothing happens until it becomes a subconscious mind belief system.

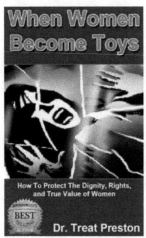

Why is character more important than reputation? Because character is more likely than not a FRAUD! Character is not! Character is the real you; reputation is not the real you. How far do you really think you will get with people once they discover your reputation doesn't match your character? One of the things we study quite intensely at AppliedMindSciences.com is gender relationships and why they succeed or fail. In fact, I just published a book a little while back called "When Women Become Toys" and it is a real eye opener. Are you failing in relationships? Go to AppliedMindSciences.com and see why.

Please remember: Character defines you; reputation just describes you in a way of your choosing. Any publicist or PR firm can make you into a god; but your true character had better match it.

You Can Focus, But Will You?

You have the ability to focus, but will you? You can, but whether you will or not depends on you. It is one thing to be able to do something, and another thing to do it.

There is far more ability not used than is used. Why do not more men of ability make something of themselves? There are comparatively few successful men but many ambitious ones. Why do not more get along?

Cases may differ, but the fault is usually their own. They have had chances, perhaps better ones than some others that have made good.

What would you like to do, that you are not doing? If you think you should be "getting on" better, why don't you? Study yourself carefully. Learn your shortcomings.

Sometimes only a mere trifle keeps one from branching out and becoming a success.

Discover why you have not been making good - the cause of your failure. Have you been expecting someone to lead you, or to make a way for you? If you have, then focus on a new line of thought.

There are two things absolutely necessary for success - energy and the will to succeed. Nothing can take the place of either of these. Most of us will not have an easy path to follow so don't expect to find one.

The hard knocks develop our courage and moral stamina. The persons that live in an indolent and slipshod way never have any. They have never faced conditions and therefore don't know how. The world is no better for their living.

We must make favorable conditions and not expect them to shape themselves. It is not the man that says, "It can't be done," but the man that goes ahead in spite of adverse advice, and shows that "it can be done" that "gets there" today. "The Lord helps those that help themselves," is a true saying.

A Stumbling Block or Stepping Stone?

Romans 14:13-23

We climb the road to success by overcoming obstacles. **Stumbling blocks are but stepping stones** for the man that says, "I can and I will." When we see cripples, the deaf and dumb, the blind and those with other handicaps amounting to something in the world, the able-bodied man should feel ashamed of himself if he does not make good.

There is nothing that can resist the force of perseverance. The way ahead of all of us is not clear sailing, but all hard passages can be bridged, if you just think they can and Focus on how to do it.

But if you think the obstacles are insurmountable, you will not of course try, and even if you do, it will be in only a half-hearted way--a way that accomplishes nothing.

Many men will not begin an undertaking unless they feel sure they will succeed in it. What a mistake! This would be right, if we were sure of what we could and could not do. But who knows? There may be an obstruction there now that might not be there next week. There may not be an obstruction there now that will be there next week.

The trouble with most persons is that just as soon as they see their way blocked they lose courage. They forget that usually there is a way around the difficulty. It's up to you to find it. If you tackle something with little effort, when the conditions call for a big effort, you will of course not win.

Tackle everything with a feeling that you will utilize all the power within you to make it a success. This is the kind of focused effort that succeeds.

Most people are beaten before they start. They think they are going to encounter obstacles, and they look for them instead of for means to overcome them. The result is that they increase their obstacles instead of diminishing them.

Have you ever undertaken something that you thought would be hard, but afterwards found it to be easy? That is the way a great many times. The things that look difficult in advance turn out to be easy of conquest when once encountered.

So start out on your journey with the idea that the road is going to be clear for you and that if it is not you will clear the way. All men that have amounted to anything have cleared their way and they did not have the assistance that you will have today.

> **It is possible to succeed and enjoy your life despite the most difficult circumstances.**

The one great keynote of success is to do whatever you have decided on. Don't be turned from your path, but resolve that you are going to accomplish what you set out to do. Don't be frightened at a few rebuffs, for they cannot stop the man that is determined - the man that knows in his heart that success is only bought by tremendous resolution, by focused and whole-hearted effort.

"He who has a firm will," says Goethe, "molds the world to himself."

"People do not lack strength," says Victor Hugo; "they lack will."

It is not so much skill that wins victories as it is activity and great determination.

There is no such thing as failure for the man that does what is required.

Never believe the lie – "I have done my best…"

You must always do what is required! This is truth!

Corporate
Protect

** Bonus **

Watch our FREE 56-minute ForensicsNation Online Public Awareness Seminar that will truly open your eyes to what you are facing with cyber crime. Go here to view the view the seminar: http://www.AddMeInNow.com

Protecting Your Business from Cyber Criminals

"Tell me; where is cyberspace? Point out to me exactly where it is. Show me the billion of airwaves coursing through our bodies and surroundings non-stop 24/7.

You have a website? Reach out and touch it for me. Reach out and pluck a fax from the air. Or reach out and pluck the photo of your kid that you just sent grandma out of the air and show it to me.

Where is the Internet? And where are the billions of bits of information sent at seemingly light speed around the world. Show them to me.

The text message you sent...where did it go and how did it get there? Show me the software you just downloaded and installed on your computer. Not the interface that pops up on your computer screen but show me the bits and bytes that make it work.

It is all AIR!!! It is nothing more than air. Every day we all buy, send and use air and every day we all do not realize that our lives are changing as new technology is released and as becomes a major part of our lives."

And sometimes the air is polluted!

Give me 30-minutes and I can turn your life into a living HELL

In 30-minutes I can:

- Access your bank accounts and steal your money

- Tap your cell phone; listen to your phone calls, read your text messages.
- I can track your movements using GPS
- I can learn all about you – where you live, where you work, your habits, if you are single or married, your kid's names and ages, EVERYTHING!
- I can access your social media and change your profile and pics
- I can post false information about you that will never come off the net.
- I can find out your religious affiliation, voting records, and more.
- I will know your car, license info, and insurance data.

In short, give me 30-minutes and I will know everything about you and you cannot stop me because all of this info is on the Internet and you will never know it is me because I can hide where nobody will find me.

Computer vs. Internet Forensics

The widespread use of computer forensics resulted from the convergence of two factors: the increasing dependence of law enforcement on computing (as in the area of fingerprints) and the ubiquity of computers that followed from the microcomputer revolution. As computer forensics evolved, it was modeled after the basic investigative methodologies of law enforcement and the security industry that championed its use.

Not surprisingly, computer forensics is about the "preservation, identification, extraction, documentation and interpretation of computer data." In order to accomplish these goals, there are well-defined procedures, also derived from law enforcement, for acquiring and analyzing the evidence without damaging it and authenticating the evidence and providing a chain-of-custody that will hold up in court.

The tools for the "search-and-seizure" side of computer forensics are a potpourri of sophisticated tools that are primarily focused on the physical side of computing: i.e., tracing and locating computer hardware, recovering hidden data from storage media, identifying and recovering hidden data, decrypting files, decompressing data, cracking passwords, "crowbarring" an operating system (bypassing normal security controls and permissions), and so forth. For those who are old enough to remember the original Norton Utilities for DOS think of these modern tools as the original Norton Disk Editor for DOS on steroids.

Listed below are some common categories and a few examples of computer forensics toolkits:

- File Viewers: Quick View Plus (http://www.jasc.com)
- Image Viewers: ThumbsPlus http://www.cerious.com)
- Password Crackers: l0phtcrack or LC4 (http://www.atstake.com)
- Format-independent Text Search: dtsearch (http://www.dtsearch.com)

- Drive Imaging: Norton Utilities' Ghost (http://www.symantec.com)
- Complete Computer Forensics Toolkits:
- Forensics Toolkit (http://www.foundstone.com);
- ForensiX (http://www.all.net);
- EnCase Forensic (http://www.encase.com)
- Forensic Computer Systems: Forensic-Computers (http://www.forensic-computers.com)
- One of the more full-featured network tools, NetScanTools Pro (http://www.netscantools.com) Note the abundance of features built into one product!

Internet Forensics specialist uses many of the same tools and engages in the same set of practices as the person he/she is investigating. Let me illustrate with a few examples. Suppose that you've received some suspicious email, and want to verify the authenticity of a URL included within. A number of options are available. One might use a browser to access information from the American Registry for Internet Numbers (http://www.arin.net). Or one might use any number of OS utilities. But we'll save ourselves some time and worry, and use a general network appliance, NetScanTools Pro. We identified the registration, domain name servers, currency information, etc. for netscantools.com.

Now let's change the scenario slightly. Suppose that we had some hostile intent, and wanted to ferret out information about some company's network infrastructure. What tool might we use? You guessed it, NetScanTools Pro. The point is that the self-same tool is equally useful to the hacker conducting basic network reconnaissance and the legitimate Internet security specialist who's trying to determine whether a URL links to a legitimate company or a packet "booby trap." The point is that, both uses require essentially the same skill sets.

In Internet Forensics it is customarily the case that the forensic specialist undergoes the same level of education and training as the hacker he or she seeks to thwart. The difference is one of ethics, not skill. We observed that this was not true of the perpetrator and investigator in computer forensics.

To drive home the point, look at the other options that NetScanTools Pro provides. One can use an ICMP "ping" to identify whether a particular network host is online just as easily as one can use it to identify activity periods in network reconnaissance or a network topology. One can use a Traceroute to determine network bottlenecks, or to identify intervening routers and gateways for possible man-in-the-middle attacks. One can use Port Probe to verify that a firewall is appropriately configured, or to make a list of vulnerable services on a host that may be exploited.

Where computer forensics deals with physical things, Internet forensics deals with the ephemeral. The computer forensics specialist at least has something to seize and investigate. The Internet forensics specialist only has something to investigate if the packet filters, firewalls and intrusion detection systems were set up to anticipate the breach of security. But, if one could always anticipate the breach, one could always block it. Therein lays the art, and the mystery.

If I've been successful, I've got you thinking about the fundamental differences between computer forensics and internet forensics. I think that on careful analysis, one has to conclude (a) that these are fundamentally different skills, (b) that in the case of Internet forensics, the skill sets of the successful perpetrator and successful investigator are pretty much the same, and (c) Internet forensics is as much a discipline as its search-and-seizure counterpart. This validity of these conclusions may be confirmed in any number of ways. For the most part the tools-of-the-trade for both hacker and Internet forensics specialist are the same, though the occasional extreme case like Dug Song's Dsniff http://monkey.org/~dugsong/dsniff challenges this generalization. It's hard for me to imagine a legitimate, lawful use of Dsniff's "macof" utility that enables the users to flood switch state tables! But in the main, the hacker and the Internet Forensics specialist could co-exist with the same tools and equipment.

Statistics on Internet Fraud

The Internet Crime Complaint Center (IC3), a joint venture of the FBI and the National White Collar Crime Center found:

- Online auction fraud was the most reported type of fraud and accounted for 44.9% of consumers' complaints

- Non-delivered merchandise and/or payment made up 19.0% of complaints

- Check fraud represented 4.9% of complaints

- About 70% of the fraud victims were scammed through www (e.g. online auctions)

- About 30% of the victims were scammed by emails

Payment Methods

Top methods of payment used by victims of Internet fraud include: Wire, Credit Card, Bank Debit, Money Order, and Check

The average loss for all Internet frauds was $1,500. More than half of these losses occurred through auctions. So protect yourself from becoming the next victim of an auction fraud. Read the tips on how to prevent auction frauds from happening to you.

Tips on How to Prevent Auction Frauds

- Learn as much as you can from the seller

- Read and examine the feedback on the seller

- Check the location of the seller. If the seller is abroad and a problem arises it will be harder to solve.

- Ask if shipping and delivery are included in the price so you receive no unexpected or additional costs.

- Refuse to give the seller your social security number or driver's license number to prevent identity theft. In fact get used to saying "no" to information requests on the Internet.

How do hackers and crackers do it?

With the advent of the internet, online information is becoming more and more prevalent without the person or entity even knowing their information is listed online.

Two of the main culprits are the following:

1. **Epsilon: http://www.epsilon.com**

2. Acxiom: http://www.acxiom.com

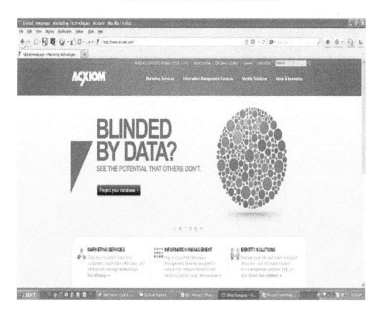

The two companies above are called "data miners" and they scour the net for your personal information. They

83

then sell this information to mostly legitimate businesses seeking to sell you goods and services but they also sell to hackers and crackers. No, not on purpose; they are duped just like you but nevertheless they do sell your info to people who should not have it.

People like Hackman1…in the summer of 2008, a hacker known as "Hackman1" began illegally accessing various corporate databases and stealing personal and financial data in order to commit identity theft. In the course of a 6-month investigation, he was responsible for over 5566 victims totaling over $15-million in damages. When he was apprehended, he was on a yacht off the Florida Keys committing more identity theft.

How bad is it? Listen…

Index of Resources

If some links are broken, please notify me at support@epubwealth.com so they can either be fixed or replaced…thanks!!!

Cell Phones
Unlock or "Jail Break your cell phone: http://bit.ly/pizQvj

Prepaidonline: http://bit.ly/o8uSPs

CellHub: http://bit.ly/odI6Md

LetsTalk: http://bit.ly/rik2Qm

RingCentral: http://bit.ly/ntIPay

Google Voice: http://www.google.com/voice

Cell Phone Spyware: http://j.mp/r2PUWK

PhoneSale: http://bit.ly/pHYVB9

GSM Nation: http://bit.ly/nfvJFF

StraightTalk: http://www.straighttalk.com

Forward your voicemail: http://bit.ly/pHYVB9

Computer
Anonymouse: http://anonymouse.org/

Hide MY IP: http://bit.ly/ow4WZD

Identity Cloaker: http://bit.ly/ofl1rs

Anonymizer: http://bit.ly/oJGbzF

NameCheap: http://bit.ly/8MgJ2

GoDaddy: http://bit.ly/p9k32w

Eset: http://www.eset.com/us/.

KillDisk: http://www.killdisk.com/

Credit
Equifax: http://www.equifax.com/home/en_us

Transunion: http://www.transunion.com/

Experian: http://www.experian.com/

Email
Hushmail: http://www.hushmail.com/

Encryption
Endoacustica: http://www.endoacustica.com/

OpenPGP: http://www.openpgp.org/

Financial
eBillme: http://www.ebillme.com/.

A   Visa   Buxx:
http://usa.visa.com/personal/cards/prepaid/visa_buxx.htm
l

Visa reloadable card:

http://usa.visa.com/personal/cards/prepaid/prepaidcard.js
p?it=l2|/personal/cards/prepaid/visa_buxx.html|Visa%20
Reloadable

GoldMoney: http://www.goldmoney.com

Firewall
Comodo: http://www.comodo.com.

GPS
GPS Locator: http://www.world-tracker.com/v4/

Mail

Forward your postal mail: http://www.earthclassmail.com/.

OptoutScreen http://www.optoutscreen.com/

CatalogChoice: https://www.catalogchoice.org

DMA Off Mailing: http://www.dmaconsumers.org/cgi/offmailing

Medical
Check your medical records: http://www.mib.com or call 866-692-6901

Miscellaneous
Free Survival Guide: http://www.neternatives.com/Products/BePreparedtoSurvive.aspx

Survival Information:

http://survivalnations.com

ProxyHeaven: http://proxy-heaven.blogspot.com/.

Phone
Skype: http://www.skype.com/;

Zfone: http://zfoneproject.com/.

Xmeeting: http://xmeeting.sourceforge.net/pages/xmeeting.php

MagicJack: http://www.magicjack.com/

Private Phone Carrier – DPI: http://www.dpiteleconnect.com/public/

Social Mobile Messaging - Jangl: http://www.jangl.com/

Rights
Security

Brickhouse Security: http://bit.ly/oTILKo

Surveillance
Find Camera Locations: http://www.photoenforced.com/

Fight   Red-Light   Cameras:
http://www.highwayrobbery.net/

Web
StartPage: http://www.startpage.com.

Tor Project: https://www.torproject.org/.

Pretty Good Privacy (PGP) http://www.pgpi.org/

Freenet Project: http://freenetproject.org/

Points to remember: here are some resources to help you remain private:

OptoutScreen http://www.optoutscreen.com/ allows you off dang near everything

CatalogChoice: https://www.catalogchoice.org keeps you off mailing lists.

DMA   Off   Mailing:
http://www.dmaconsumers.org/cgi/offmailing gets you off mailing lists for $1.

Acxiom is one of the worst compilers of info. Request you be removed by emailing them at optoutus@acxiom.com

Check your medical records to see if they have been compromised: http://www.mib.com or call 866-692-6901

Chapter 4 – How To Repair Any Damage Done to Your Online Reputation

Repairing your online reputation is not as difficult as it seems and I have found the following websites pretty good in their services:

http://www.officialreputationmanagement.com/
http://www.reputation.com/
http://www.removeyourname.com/

Here is a YouTube video and does an excellent job in explaining the various techniques:

Simple Steps To Track, Manage And *Repair Your Online Reputation*
http://www.youtube.com/watch?v=mds4szNYfxU

One of the sites that has proven itself is Computer Geeks and the following article explains what they do and what to do if you are attacked:

Online Reputation Repair
http://www.computer-geek.net/online-reputation-repair.htm

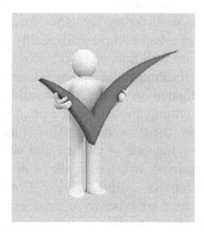

Nothing is more frustrating than finding your name or your company's name displayed in a negative light on the internet. You would be shocked to discover how easy it is for some disgruntled customer to ruin your online reputation, a reputation you may have painstakingly built over many years. Millions of internet users use search engines like Google, Bing, MSN, and Yahoo to research individuals or companies before they decide whether to do business with them. They type in your name or your company's name and all public information will then be displayed to them. If this information is negative, even if it is untrue, it can cause serious damage to your business or your personal life.

How is your reputation being ruined?
Negative comments or complaints can be posted on blogs or forums but what seems to be the most damaging is having a bad report created by "Complaint websites". These websites claim that they are doing an important service on behalf of consumers in that they allow consumers to file complaints/negative comments anonymously in the guise of protecting other consumers from what they deem as a bad company. In reality, these "Complaint websites" are well documented as companies that commit outright blackmail and slander. Complaint reports are not investigated to verify their validity so anyone can make up anything about a person or company and have it posted on these websites. Unfortunately, many people will err on the side of caution and not take the chance of doing business with you if they run across one of these false reports online. Aside from the "Complaint websites", here are other avenues where your online reputation can take a beating: negative comments in Google, Bing, Yahoo etc; poor reviews/ratings in local directory websites or in City guides; forums, social

networking websites (Facebook, LinkedIn, etc.); negative videos on YouTube; Industry-specific internet portals; Online Yellow pages; Online News stories.

How to repair your online reputation?
Erasing negative comments is not easy. You could try contacting the appropriate people and respectfully ask that a negative comment be removed but that certainly doesn't mean that they will. It would be almost impossible to track down anonymous culprits behind offending material and negative comments posted on forum and blogs are considered free speech with no one being accountable. Even if you can pinpoint the offender, the cost of dragging them through the courts is usually not worth it.

The most effective and popular way to go about repairing your online reputation is to promote and circulate positive information in order to bury the negative information. You start a campaign to get the "good" word out about your company mainly by "link building". Positive website promotion with Link building will push the negative page or pages off the first few pages of Google, Bing, Yahoo and MSN, essentially "burying" it and replacing it with positive information about your company.

You can promote your website positively through the following ways:
- Release high visibility Press Releases that highlight achievements, awards, public service etc.

- Submit custom-written articles to all major article publishing websites
- Have blogs that post dozens of positive reviews to counteract the negative
- Create web pages promoting specific positive points about your company
- It is important to take action immediately if you spot negative information on the internet. The longer you put off doing something about it, the more links and connections these negative pages will build to other websites. Bad news travels really fast on the Internet.

If you are serious in your need to clean up damaging information about yourself or your company, your best bet would be to employ a Reputation Repair company rather than try to tackle the job yourself. Google has a very powerful and complicated infrastructure, with a very detailed and specific formula for how information is ranked within the search results, and unless you are an expert in SEO, it is best to leave it to the experts.

Contact The Computer Geeks to talk about what we can do to protect your online reputation. We would be happy to present an estimate free of charge.

Contact Us:
sales@computer-geek.net
905-426-1784

*****

For those of you who wish to tackle correcting your online reputation yourself use the following Word of

Mouth Marketing websites to spread the good words about you:

Word of Mouth Marketing Websites
http://mylikes.com/
http://www.extole.com/
http://izea.com/
http://sponsoredtweets.com/
http://socialspark.com/
http://wereward.com/
http://inpostlinks.com/
https://payperpost.com/
https://www.reviewme.com/

http://www.amazon.com/dp/B006X0FXU8

Most people are not aware of WOMM in marketing let alone in online reputation repair. I actually use them daily to spread the word about my books and I can tell you honestly they are very effective.

I also use outsourcing sites as follows:

http://www.replacemyself.com/
http://123employee.com/
http://www.elance.com/
http://www.agentsofvalue.com/
http://www.guru.com/index.aspx
http://www.allfreelance.com/
http://www.agentsofvalue.com/
http://www.microworkers.com/
http://www.taskrabbit.com
https://www.odesk.com/
http://www.skillwho.com/
http://www.contentnetwork.com/
http://www.warriorforum.com/warriors-hire/
http://www.getafreelancer.com

I have highlighted both microworkers and Taskrabbit above because I tend to use these two sites the most. You can hire online workers and inexpensive prices to post good stuff about you.

Now let's move on to the Dos and Don'ts of Internet Usage…

Chapter 5 – The DOs and DON'TS of Internet Usage

The following was written by A.J. Surin and although he is writing to a Malaysian audience, what he writes applies to the United States too. The complete White Paper can be found here:

http://www.crime-research.org/library/Cybercriminal.html

To catch a cybercriminal
By A.J. Surin

WHAT is cybercrime? The Oxford Reference Online defines cybercrime as crime committed over the Internet

http://www.oxfordreference.com/views/ENTRY.html?ssid=175131518&entry=t49.000925&srn=1&category=-FIRSTHIT

Some people call cybercrime "computer crime." The Encyclopedia Britannica defines computer crime as any crime that is committed by means of special knowledge or expert use of computer technology.

Computer crime could reasonably include a wide variety of criminal offences, activities, or issues. The scope of the definition becomes even larger with the frequent companion or substitute term "computer-related crime." Some writers are also of the opinion that "computer crime" refers to computer-related activities which are either criminal in the legal sense of the word or just antisocial behavior where there is no breach of the law (Lee, M.K.O. (1995) Legal control of computer crime in Hong Kong, Information Management & Computer Security 3(2) 13-19 –

http://mustafa.emeraldlibrary.com/vl=4775179/cl=50/nw=1/rpsv/~1177/v3n2/s3/p13)

The word "hacker" should also be defined here, as it will be used extensively in this article – hackers are basically people who break into and tamper with computer information systems. The word "cracker" carries a similar meaning, and "cracking" means to decipher a code, password or encrypted message.

What is concerning is that organized crime is escalating on the Internet, according to a 2002 statement by the head of Britain's National High-tech Crime Unit, Lee Hynds (www.ananova.com/news/story/sm_724492.html?menu). According to him the Internet provides organized crime groups with "a relatively low risk theatre of operations."

As the topic of cybercrime is so wide, what I would like to do is focus on Malaysia's Computer Crimes Act 1997, local law enforcement and practical tips on how to prevent cybercrime.

Computer crime laws in other countries, the enforcement and multilateral efforts to harmonies laws against cybercrime will be discussed in next month's column.

Are there laws in Malaysia to prosecute cybercriminals? What are the penalties for cybercriminals in Malaysia?

The need for laws against cybercriminals is obvious. A school dropout from the Philippines who wrote the ILOVEYOU virus was not prosecuted by the Philippine Government because at that time, the country did not have laws relating to virus creators. Ironically, the then President Estrada stated that perhaps the Philippines should leverage on the fact that they have such good virus writers to attract global technology companies to base themselves in the Philippines, considering the capable talent available in the country.

Viruses and worms are getting more insidious nowadays – take for instance, the Swen worm, which cleverly disguises itself as an e-mail message from Microsoft with a patch attached.

Illegal uses

Besides hacking and cracking, technology and the Internet can be used for a myriad of other illegal purposes: drug dealers use encrypted fax machines to send orders for narcotics to their suppliers in a neighboring country.

Gangsters can use computers for extortion. Prostitution rings maintain their customer payments and client lists through computer software applications. Burglary rings track break-ins and then inventory their winnings from each job. Gangsters who want to murder a person in hospital can crack the hospital's computers to alter the dosage of medication

http://www.scmagazine.com/scmagazine/2000_04/cover/cover.html

Cybercriminals can range from teenagers who vandalize websites to terrorists who target a nation. However, we will leave the discussion on cyberterrorism to another installation of this column.
Laws specifically catered for criminal activity through, over and using the Internet is essential for a nation state to have, especially in this globalised, Internet age. Take the example of the ILOVEYOU virus again, which spread to at least 45 million computers worldwide causing billions of dollars in damage.

100

The Computer Crimes Act 1997 provides for offences against cybercrime. Now, it is not the case that the other Acts of Parliament do not provide for criminal offences (like the Communications and Multimedia Act 1998, the Digital Signature Act 1997 and the Optical Discs Act 2000), it is just that in terms of cybercrime itself, the Act of Parliament which is the most relevant is the Computer Crimes Act. This Act is divided into three parts that is the "Preliminary," "Offences" and "Ancillary and General Provisions" parts and is 12 sections long. It came into force on June 1, 2000.

Section 3 provides for the offence of unauthorized access to computer material. A person shall be guilty of an offence if three elements exist, that is:

- He causes a computer to perform any function with intent to secure access to any program or data held in any computer;
- The access he intends to secure is unauthorized; and
- He knows at the time that he accesses the computer without authorization.

The section then states that the intent a person has to have to commit the offence need not be directed at any particular program or data, a program or data of any particular kind or a program or data held in any particular computer. One meaning of this part may be that it does not matter whether or not a hacker knows what the consequences of his act will be, which program or data he

101

or she will access or even which computer he or she will access, just as long as he knows that his access is unauthorized. The penalty for this offence is a maximum fine of RM 50,000, a maximum prison sentence of five years or both the fine and imprisonment.

Section 4 provides for the offence of unauthorized access with intent to commit or facilitate the commission of a further offence. A person shall be guilty of an offence under this section if two elements exist, that is:

- He or she accesses unauthorized computer material without access; and
- He or she accesses this computer material with the intent of: committing an offence involving fraud or dishonesty or which causes injury as defined in the Penal Code; or facilitating the commission of such an offence whether by himself or by any other person.

A person guilty of an offence under this section shall on conviction be liable to a maximum fine of RM 150,000 or a maximum prison term of 10 years or both the fine and imprisonment. As you can see, the legislature has provided for a higher fine and a higher prison term for this offence, as the crime here is more serious than in Section 3, as the commission of a further offence of fraud, dishonesty or injury is envisaged.

Unauthorized modification

Section 5 provides for the offence of unauthorized modification of the contents of any computer. A person shall be guilty of the offence if he does any act which he knows will cause unauthorized modification of the contents of any computer. Section 5 also states that it is immaterial that the act in question is not directed at any particular program or data a program or data of any kind or a program or data held in any particular computer.

This most probably means that it does not matter whether or not the hacker knows which program or data, or even which computer will be affected by his actions, just as long as he knows his actions will cause unauthorized modifications. For the purposes of Section 5, it is immaterial whether an unauthorized modification is, or is intended to be, permanent or merely temporary. The penalty is a maximum fine of RM 100,000 or a maximum prison sentence of seven years or both the fine and prison sentence. However, if the modification was done to cause injury, then the maximum fine is RM 150,000 and the maximum prison term is 10 years.

Section 6 is the offence of wrongful communication. A person shall be guilty of an offence if he communicates directly or indirectly a number, code, password or other means of access to a computer to any person other than a person to whom he is duly authorized to communicate it to. The penalty for the offence is a maximum fine of RM 25,000 or a maximum prison sentence of three years or both.

Section 7 provides for a criminal offence if a person assists in the commissioning of any of the offences above, attempts to commit any of the offences above or was preparing to commit any of the offences above.

Section 11 provides for the criminal offence if:

- A person assaults, obstructs, hinders or delays a police officer when the latter is attempting to enter any premises for the purposes searching, seizing or arresting as provided for under the Act; or

- A person fails to comply with any lawful demands of a police officer acting in the execution of his duty under the Act.

A person found guilty under Section 11 faces a maximum fine of RM 25,000 or a maximum prison term of three years or to both the fine and prison term.

Section 9 of the Computer Crimes Act states that the provisions of the Act shall have effect outside as well as within Malaysia and where the commission of the offence was performed outside Malaysia, he may be dealt with in respect of such offence as if it was committed at a place within Malaysia. Section 9 goes on to state that the Act shall apply if, for the offence in question, the computer, program or data was in Malaysia or capable of being connected to or sent to or used by or with a computer in Malaysia at the material time.

This practically means that the Computer Crimes Act has extra-territorial jurisdiction – the law can be enforced against an alleged offender even if he is in another country.

One more interesting thing about the Act is that Section

10 gives the power to any police officer to arrest without warrant any person whom he (the police officer) reasonably believes to have committed or is committing an offence under the Act.

Thus, the police have sweeping powers of arrest with regards to cybercrime and reflect the legislature's consideration that it viewed the offences in the Act as pretty serious.

Practical examples of cybercrime

Some people may argue that there is a difference between hackers who break into a website to deface its homepage and cyberterrorists who go to these same websites with the purpose of causing harm to people and damage to databases and information systems (see for instance Lee, M.K.O. (1995) above). However, if you look at Section 5 of the Act carefully, Malaysian law does not make a distinction between a harmless hacker who defaces a webpage and a cyberterrorist who desires to cause injury – both will be guilty of offences under the Act, and both will be punishable, although by different sections of the Act.

Practical examples of cybercrimes include but are not limited to:

Cyberstalking: The goal of a cyberstalker is control. Stalking and harassment over cyberspace is more easily practiced than in real life. There are many cases where cyberstalking crosses over to physical stalking.

Some examples of computer harassment are:

- Live chat obscenities and harassment;
- Unsolicited and threatening e-mail;
- Hostile postings about someone;
- Spreading vicious rumors about someone;
- Leaving abusive messages on a website's guest books.

Cases where the crime can occur even if there was no computer – however, the use of technology makes the commission of the crime faster and permits the processing of larger amounts of information. Examples would be credit card fraud, drug trafficking, criminal breach of trust, forgery, cheating, illegal betting or gambling, forgery of valuable documents (money, checks, passports and identification cards) and money laundering. In the past, the Malaysian Police has investigated rumour mongering and defamation on the Internet.

Malicious codes like worms, viruses and Trojan horses: These exploit security vulnerabilities of a system and they tend to alter or destroy data. The damage they cost is worth millions of Ringgit to companies as well as government agencies. Worms are different from viruses because they are able to spread themselves with no user interaction. A virus can attack systems in many ways: by erasing files, corrupting databases and destroying hard disk drives.

Hacking: Hacked systems can be used for information gathering, information alteration, and sabotage. Vulnerabilities exist in almost every network. Hackers

106

sometime crack into systems to brag about their abilities to penetrate into systems, but others do it for illegal gain or other malicious purposes. Today, hacking is simpler than ever – hackers can now go to websites and download protocols, programs and scripts to use against their victims.

Cyberterrorism: This is the premeditated, politically motivated attack against information, computer systems, computer programs, and data which result in violence against noncombatant targets. We shall discuss cyberterrorism as a separate topic as this is an area of special concern and because certain countries have legislated on the topic.

Industrial espionage: This is where corporations spy on other companies and with network systems; this can be an easy task. Companies can retrieve sensitive information rarely leaving behind any evidence. Cyberespionage can also be applied to nations that spy on other countries' sensitive information.

Spoofing of IP addresses. This is where a false IP address is used to impersonate an authorized user.

The reproduction and distribution of copyright protected material and software piracy

Cyberattacks on financial systems: This includes electronic banking and payment systems.

Cybervandalism: The defacing of webpages.

Pyramid schemes on the Internet.

E-mail abuse: This includes malicious or false e-mail.

Denial of service attacks.

Who are the local enforcers – what type of enforcement do we have in Malaysia?

Cyberlaw enforcers face several challenges:

Firstly, there is the identification of the criminal – Internet investigations are equipment- and labor-intensive. It is not that easy to identify cybercriminals.

This is because they operate in a virtual world and do not leave physical clues and paper trails behind, like the more traditional criminals do. Although they do leave their digital fingerprints now and then, enforcers need to move quickly before evidence fades away. Furthermore, with encryption, route relay and other types of technology and processes, they can make themselves almost undetectable by cyberenforcers.

Secondly, if the cybercriminal was in another country and he perpetrated his crimes against information systems here in Malaysia, how do you prosecute and ultimately impose the sentence against him? This is where the harmonization of a framework of cyberlaw globally will undoubtedly help (this was discussed in the Cyberlaws column in In.Tech, April 22. It is also the objective in respect to cyberlaw in the second phase of the MSC's development from 2003 to 2010), as the Internet is borderless and does not have regard to the laws of sovereign nations.

Insufficient Personnel

Besides legal differences, there are practical differences in terms of enforcement and co-ordination efforts between nations. There may not be enough trained personnel or sufficient equipment to detect and to bring cybercriminals to book.

Finally, technology always evolves and the enforcers must keep up with changes. Even in the United States as recently as 2000, it was noted that American law enforcement agencies, including the Justice Department, lacked the staff to investigate and prosecute cybercrimes like digital break-ins, data destruction and viruses. As a result of this, cybercriminals were breaking into or paralyzing US-based websites with little fear of retribution, costing the private sector hundreds of millions of dollars.

Even Interpol, the organization set up to track fugitives and investigate international crime and of which Malaysia is a member of, considered letting a Silicon Valley computer security company, AtomicTangerine, help it to protect businesses from hackers. This is after it acknowledged that international law enforcers were unable to combat computer crime effectively and also after acknowledging that governments found it difficult to coordinate cross-border efforts to combat this new phenomenon. Its secretary general at the time, Raymond Kendall stated that "... there's a limit to how you can

109

transform police officers or detectives into technicians" (http://lists.insecure.org/lists/isn/2000/Jul/0056.html).

In Malaysia, the Malaysian Police formed the Technology Crime Investigation Branch (TCIB) in October 1998. It is under the Commercial Crime Investigation Division. The officers in the TCIB are specially trained in cybercriminal investigation methods. The TCIB also lends its assistance to overseas enforcement agencies in investigating online gambling, hacking and illegal distribution of pirated software.

Here are a couple of tips on how to prevent cybercrime:

- Install hardware and software that will recognise hacker attacks, data spying and data altering, like firewalls, encryption (for e-mail, the encryption program called Pretty Good Privacy can be used), virus detection and smartcards. An Intrusion Detection System can protect your information systems in the event of the failure of the firewall and from internal attacks. An Incident Handling System will be able to identify hacker attacks as they happen. Full backups are important so that evidence like damaged or altered files, files left by the intruder, the relevant IP address and login times can be collected. A police report should then be made.

- Assess your information systems to identify weaknesses.

- Ensure that computers that run critical infrastructure are not physically connected to any other computer that is possibly connected to the Internet.

- Maintain clear and consistent security policies and procedures.

- Use alphanumeric passwords (i.e. passwords with letters and numbers in them). Login passwords should be changed frequently.

- Employees have to be trained to understand security risks – this practically means that they must know that they should never give out PINs, passwords and calling card numbers of the company without proper third party verification.

Notorious hacker, Kevin Mitnick, who was the most wanted hacker at one time in the United States, told of how he accessed the information systems of the US' Department of Motor Vehicles by simply calling up an officer, disguising himself as an officer from another government agency and obtaining the appropriate username and passwords from her.

- Correct identified problems – although this may seem straightforward and logical, I have seen many cases where security of certain information systems was compromised because problems were not fixed.

- Report attacks to the National ICT Security and Emergency Response Centre (Niser) so that any pattern of cybercrime in Malaysia can be detected and large-scale attacks prevented.

- There must exist incident response capabilities so that there is appropriate action taken against impending attacks.

- When an employee resigns or is terminated, employers must always ensure that the former does not have access to their computers anymore. The 1997 UN Manual on the Prevention and Control of Computer-Related Crime noted that 90% of economic crimes such as theft of information and fraud were committed by the relevant company's employees. Even the Malaysian Police's Technology Crime Investigation Branch is of the opinion that "more often than not, unauthorized access, hacking or e-mail abuse cases involve disgruntled employees taking advantage of ineffective security policies."

- Maintain backups of all important data.

- When external persons service your system, save confidential information on other media before the service. Observe them during the service. Never let external people take computers or servers with confidential information from your site.

Conclusion

In a speech in Kuala Lumpur in February 2000, Deputy Prime Minister Datuk Seri Abdullah Ahmad Badawi stated that: "The development of the Multimedia Super Corridor and the creation of a pioneer legal and regulatory framework encompassing, amongst other things, the Communications and Multimedia Act, the Computer Crimes Act and the Digital Signatures Act is indicative of the Government's commitment towards the creation of a knowledge-based economy." *(The Harvard Business School Alumni Club luncheon talk on Managing Malaysia in the New Global Economy.)*

Thus, the Computer Crimes Act must be seen not only as a law which regulates the behavior of people who use and do business over the Internet, but it also must be seen as the Government's efforts to put in place soft infrastructure to nurture the MSC and the knowledge-based economy so that Malaysia can achieve Vision 2020. At the same time, the Government should be aware that technological innovation and the deviousness of human minds would mean that the law as well as enforcement must not only keep up with cybercriminals, but it must ensure that their officers are one step ahead of cybercriminals, ready to catch them if the cybercriminals perform their dirty deeds.

Chapter 6 – Using Social Media with Caution

Key Danger Signs to Look For In Online Social Media Sites

Now I am going to teach you criminal profiling and how to spot fraud artist simply by the words they use and how they structure their content.

*****

Gender-Sensitive Language
What is "gender-sensitive language" and why should I use it?

English speakers and writers have traditionally been taught to use masculine nouns and pronouns in situations where the gender of their subject(s) is unclear or variable, or when a group to which they are referring contains members of both sexes. For example, the U.S. Declaration of Independence states that " . . . all men are created equal . . ." and most of us were taught in elementary school to understand the word "men" in that context includes both male and female Americans. In recent decades, however, as women have become increasingly involved in the public sphere of American life, writers have reconsidered the way they express gender identities and relationships. Because most English language readers no longer understand the word "man" to be synonymous with "people," writers today must think more carefully about the ways they express gender in order to convey their ideas clearly and accurately to their readers.

NOTE: *This is important. Con artists write their content most often ignoring gender identity. They consistently use the word "man" to refer to both men and women.*

115

Moreover, these issues are important for people concerned about issues of social inequality. There is a relationship between our language use and our social reality. If we "erase" women from language, that makes it easier to maintain gender inequality. As Professor Sherryl Kleinman (2000:6) has argued,

[M]ale-based generics are another indicator—and, more importantly, a *reinforcer*—of a system in which "man" in the abstract and men in the flesh are privileged over women.

Words matter and our language choices have consequences. If we believe that women and men deserve social equality, then we should think seriously about how to reflect that belief in our language use.

You're probably already aware that tackling gender sensitivity in your writing is no small task, especially since there isn't yet (and there may never be) a set of concrete guidelines on which to base your decisions. Fortunately, there are a number of different strategies the gender-savvy writer can use to express gender relationships with precision.

Pronouns

A pronoun is a word that substitutes for a noun. The English language provides pronoun options for references to masculine nouns (for example, "he" can substitute for "Tom"), feminine nouns ("she" can replace "Lucy"), and neutral/non-human nouns ("it" stands in for "a tree"), but no choice for sex-neutral third-person singular nouns ("the writer," "a student," or "someone"). Although most of us learned in elementary school that masculine pronouns (he, his, him) should be used as the "default" in situations where the referent (that is, the person or thing to which you're referring) could be either male or female, that usage is generally considered unacceptable now. So what should you do when you're faced with one of those gender-neutral or gender-ambiguous situations? Well, you've got a few options:

1. Use "they"

This option is currently much debated by grammar experts, but most agree that it works well in at least several kinds of situations. In order to use "they" to express accurately gender relationships, you'll need to understand that "they" is traditionally used only to refer to a plural noun. For example,

***Sojourner Truth and Elizabeth Cady Stanton** was famous "first-wave" American feminists. **They** were also both involved in the Abolitionist movement.*

In speech, though, we early twenty-first century Americans commonly use "they" to refer to a singular referent. According to many grammar experts, that usage is incorrect, but here's an example of how it sounds in our everyday speech:

*If **a student** wants to learn more about gender inequality, **they** should take Intro to Women's Studies.*

Note that in this example, "a student" is singular, but it is replaced in the second sentence by "they," a plural pronoun. In speech, we often don't notice such substitutions of the plural for the singular, but in writing, some will find such substitutions awkward or incorrect. Some people argue that "they" should become the default gender-neutral pronoun for English writing, but since that usage can still sound awkward to many readers, it's best to use "they" only in plural situations. Thus, one other option the gender-savvy writer may choose to employ is to make her/his sentence plural. Here's one way that can work:

A student's beliefs about feminism may be based on what **he** *has heard in the popular media...*can become...*Students' beliefs about feminism may be based on what* **they** *have heard in the popular media.*

2. Use she or he or she/he.

There is another, simpler option the gender-savvy writer can use to deal with situations where a pronoun needs to refer to a person whose gender isn't known: write out both pronoun options as "she or he" or "she/he." For example,

Each **student** *who majors in Women's Studies major must take a course in Feminist Theory.* **She or he** *may also get course credit for completing an internship at a local organization that benefits women.*

OR

*Each **student** who majors in Women's Studies major must take a course in Feminist Theory. **She/he** may also get course credit for completing an internship at a local organization that benefits women.*

3. Alternate genders and pronouns

You may also choose to alternate gendered pronouns. This option will work only in certain situations, though— usually hypothetical situations in which the referent is equally likely to be a male or a female. For example, both male and female students use the Writing Center's services, so the author of our staff manual chose to alternate between masculine and feminine pronouns when writing the following tutoring guidelines:

- Respond as a reader, explaining what and how you were/are thinking as you read her texts so that she can discover where a reader might struggle with her writing.
- Ask him to outline the draft to reveal the organization of the paper.
- Ask her to describe her purpose and audience and show how she has taken them into account in her writing.
- Explain a recurring pattern and let him locate repeated instances of it.

Of course, this author could also have included both pronouns in each sentence by writing "her/his" or "her/him," but in this case, alternating "he" and "she" conveys the same sense of gender variability and is likely a little easier on the reader, who won't have to pause to process several different options every time a gendered pronoun is needed in the sentence. This example also provides a useful demonstration of how gender-savvy writers can take advantage of the many different options available by choosing the one that best suits the unique requirements of each piece of writing they produce.

4. Eliminate the pronoun altogether

Finally, you can also simply eliminate the pronoun. For example,

Allan Johnson *is a contemporary feminist theorist. This **writer and professor** gave a speech at UNC in the fall of 2007.*

Note how the sentence used "this writer and professor" rather than "he."

Many people accept the negative stereotype that if a person is a feminist, ***she*** *must hate men...*could become...*Many people accept the negative stereotype that* ***feminist beliefs*** *are based on hatred of men.*

Note how the second version of the sentence talks about the beliefs. By avoiding using the pronoun "she," it leaves open the possibility that men may be feminists.

Gendered nouns

Like gendered pronouns, gendered nouns can also provide a stumbling block for the gender-savvy writer. The best way to avoid implications these words can carry

120

is simply to be aware of how we tend to use them in speech and writing. Because gendered nouns are so commonly used and accepted by English writers and speakers, we often don't notice them or the implications they bring with them. Once you've recognized that a gender distinction is being made by such a word, though, conversion of the gendered noun into a gender-savvy one is usually very simple.

"Man" and words ending in "-man" are the most commonly used gendered nouns, so avoiding the confusion they bring can be as simple as watching out for these words and replacing them with words that convey your meaning more effectively. For example, if the founders of America had been gender-savvy writers, they might have written " . . . all people are created equal" instead of " . . . all men are created equal . . .."

Another common gendered expression, particularly in informal speech and writing, is "you guys." This expression is used to refer to groups of men, groups of women, and groups that include both men and women. Although most people *mean* to be inclusive when they use "you guys," this phrase wouldn't make sense if it didn't subsume women under the category "guys." To see why "you guys" is gendered male, consider that "a guy" (singular) is definitely a man, not a woman, and that most men would not feel included in the expression "you gals" or "you girls."

Another example of gendered language is the way the words "Mr.," "Miss," and "Mrs." are used. "Mr." can refer to any man, regardless of whether he is single or

121

married—but women are defined by their relationship to men (by whether they are married or not). A way around this is to use "Ms." (which doesn't indicate marital status) to refer to women.

Sometimes we modify nouns that refer to jobs or positions to denote the sex of the person holding that position. This often done if the sex of the person holding the position goes against conventional expectations. To get a sense of these expectations, think about what sex you would instinctively assume the subject of each of these sentences to be:

The doctor walked into the room.

The nurse walked into the room.

Many people assume that doctors are men and that nurses are women. Because of such assumptions, someone might write sentences like "The female doctor walked into the room" or "The male nurse walked into the room." Using "female" and "male" in this way reinforces the assumption that most or all doctors are male and most or all nurses are female. Unless the sex of the nurse or doctor is important to the meaning of the sentence, it can be omitted.

As you work on becoming a gender-savvy writer, you may find it helpful to watch out for the following gendered nouns and replace them with one of the alternatives listed below. Check a thesaurus for alternatives to gendered nouns not included in this list.

gendered noun	gender-neutral noun
man	person, individual
freshman	first-year student
mankind	people, human beings, humanity
man-made	machine-made, synthetic
the common man	the average (or ordinary) person
to man	to operate, to cover, to staff
chairman	chair, chairperson, coordinator
mailman	mail carrier, letter carrier, postal worker
policeman	police officer
steward, stewardess	flight attendant
congressman	congress person, legislator, representative
Dear Sir:	Dear Sir or Madam:, Dear Editor:, Dear Service Representative:, To Whom it May Concern:

Proper nouns

Proper nouns can also give gender-savvy writers pause, but as with common nouns, it is usually very easy to use

123

gender-neutral language once you've noticed the gendered patterns in your own writing. And the best way to avoid any confusion in your use of proper nouns is to use the same rules to discuss of women subjects as you already use when you're writing about men. In the examples below, notice how using different conventions for references to male and female subjects suggests a difference in the amount of respect being given to individuals on the basis of their gender.

1. Refer to women subjects by only their last names—just as you would do for men subjects.

For example, we would never refer to William Shakespeare as just "William;" we call him "Shakespeare" or "William Shakespeare." Thus, you should never refer to Jane Austen simply as "Jane;" you should write "Jane Austen" or "Austen."

2. In circumstances where you're writing about several people who have the same last name, try using the full name of the person every time you refer to him/her.

For example, if you're writing about George and Martha Washington, referring to him as "Washington" and her as "Martha" conveys a greater respect for him than for her. In order to express an equal amount of respect for these two historical figures, simply refer to each subject by her/his full name: "George Washington" and "Martha Washington." This option may sound like it could get too wordy, but it actually works very well in most situations.

3. Refer to women subjects by their full titles, just as you would refer to men subjects.

For example, you wouldn't call American President Reagan "Ronald," so you wouldn't want to refer to British Prime Minister Thatcher as "Margaret." Simply call her "Prime Minister Thatcher," just as you would write "President Reagan" to refer to him.

Sex versus gender

In many women's studies classes, one of the fundamental concepts students are expected to master is the difference feminists see between an individual's sex (which feminists understand as one's biological makeup—male, female, or intersexed) and that person's gender (a social construction based on sex—man/masculine or woman/feminine). Because this distinction is so fundamental to understanding much of the material in many Women's Studies courses, expressing the difference between sex and gender is an important element in many writing assignments given by women's studies instructors.

Essentially, all you need to express sex vs. gender distinctions accurately in your writing is a clear understanding of the difference between sex and gender. As you are writing, ask yourself whether what you're talking about is someone's biological makeup or something about the way that person has been socialized. If you're referring to biology, use "male" or "female," and if what you're talking about has to do with a behavior or social role someone has been taught because of her/his biology, use "woman" or "man."

Thinking about the different answers to these two questions might help clarify the distinction between sex and gender:

What does it mean to be male?

What does it mean to be a man?

"To be male," as an expression of biological sex, is to have a chromosomal makeup of XY. "To be a man," however, expresses the socially constructed aspects of masculinity. Ideas of masculinity change across time, culture, and place. Think about the differences between what it meant "to be a man" in 17th-century France versus what it means "to be a man" today in the United States.

Checklist for gender revisions

To ensure that you've used gender savvy language in your piece of writing, try asking yourself the following questions:

1. Have you used "man" or "men" or words containing one of them to refer to people who may be female? If so, consider substituting another word. For example, instead of "fireman," try "firefighter."
2. If you have mentioned someone's gender, was it necessary to do so? If you identify someone as a

female architect, for example, do you (or would you) refer to someone else as a "male architect"? And if you then note that the woman is an attractive blonde mother of two, do you mention that the man is a muscular, dark-haired father of three? Unless gender and related matters—looks, clothes, parenthood—are relevant to your point, leave them unmentioned.

3. Do you use any occupational stereotypes? Watch for the use of female pronouns for elementary school teachers and male ones for scientists, for example.
4. Do you use language that in any way shows a lack of respect for either sex?
5. Have you used "he," "him," "his," or "himself" to refer to people who may be female?

*****

I want to offer the following excellent article for your perusal. I have removed the figures and illustrations but have given you the article's URL so that you can read it online, which includes the credits too.

Personality, Gender, and Age in the Language of Social Media: The Open-Vocabulary Approach

- H. Andrew Schwartz mail,
- Johannes C. Eichstaedt,
- Margaret L. Kern,
- Lukasz Dziurzynski,
- Stephanie M. Ramones,
- Megha Agrawal,
- Achal Shah,
- Michal Kosinski,

127

- David Stillwell,
- Martin E. P. Seligman,
- Lyle H. Ungar

http://www.plosone.org/article/info%3Adoi%2F10.1371%2Fjournal.pone.0073791

Abstract

We analyzed 700 million words, phrases, and topic instances collected from the Facebook messages of 75,000 volunteers, who also took standard personality tests, and found striking variations in language with personality, gender, and age. In our *open-vocabulary* technique, the data itself drives a comprehensive exploration of language that distinguishes people, finding connections that are not captured with traditional closed-vocabulary word-category analyses. Our analyses shed new light on psychosocial processes yielding results that are face valid (e.g., subjects living in high elevations talk about the mountains), tie in with other research (e.g., neurotic people disproportionately use the phrase 'sick of' and the word 'depressed'), suggest new hypotheses (e.g., an active life implies emotional stability), and give detailed insights (males use the possessive 'my' when mentioning their 'wife' or 'girlfriend' more often than females use 'my' with 'husband' or 'boyfriend'). To date, this represents the largest study, by an order of magnitude, of language and personality.

Citation: Schwartz HA, Eichstaedt JC, Kern ML, Dziurzynski L, Ramones SM, et al. (2013) Personality, Gender, and Age in the Language of Social Media: The Open-Vocabulary Approach. PLoS ONE 8(9): e73791. doi:10.1371/journal.pone.0073791

Editor: Tobias Preis, University of Warwick, United Kingdom
Received: January 23, 2013; **Accepted:** July 29, 2013; **Published:** September 25, 2013
Funding: Support for this research was provided by the Robert Wood Johnson Foundation's Pioneer Portfolio, through a grant to Martin Seligman, "Exploring Concept of Positive Health". The funders had no role in study design, data collection and analysis, decision to publish, or preparation of the manuscript.
Competing interests: The authors have declared that no competing interests exist.

Introduction

The social sciences have entered the age of data science, leveraging the unprecedented sources of written language that social media afford. Through media such as Facebook and Twitter, used regularly by more than $1/7^{th}$ of the world's population, variation in mood has been tracked diurnally and across seasons, used to predict the stock market, and leveraged to estimate happiness across time. Search patterns on Google detect influenza epidemics weeks before CDC data confirm them, and the digitization of books makes possible the quantitative tracking of cultural trends over decades. To make sense of the massive data available, multidisciplinary collaborations between fields such as computational

129

linguistics and the social sciences are needed. Here, we demonstrate an instrument which uniquely describes similarities and differences among groups of people in terms of their differential language use.

Our technique leverages what people say in social media to find distinctive *words*, *phrases*, and *topics* as functions of known attributes of people such as gender, age, location, or psychological characteristics. The standard approach to correlating language use with individual attributes is to examine usage of *a priori* fixed sets of words, limiting findings to preconceived relationships with words or categories. In contrast, we extract a data-driven collection of *words*, *phrases*, and *topics*, in which the lexicon is based on the words of the text being analyzed. This yields a comprehensive description of the differences between groups of people for any given attribute, and allows one to find unexpected results. We call approaches like ours, which do not rely on *a priori* word or category judgments, *open-vocabulary* analyses.

We use *differential language analysis* (*DLA*), our particular method of open-vocabulary analysis, to find language features across millions of Facebook messages that distinguish demographic and psychological attributes. From a dataset of over 15.4 million Facebook messages collected from 75 thousand volunteers, we extract 700 million instances of *words*, *phrases*, and automatically generated *topics* and correlate them with gender, age, and personality. We replicate traditional language analyses by applying Linguistic Inquiry and Word Count (*LIWC*), a popular tool in psychology, to our data set. Then, we show that *open-vocabulary* analyses

130

can yield additional *insights* (correlations between personality and behavior as manifest through language) and more *information* (as measured through predictive accuracy) than traditional *a priori* word-category approaches. We present a word cloud-based technique to visualize results of *DLA*. Our large set of correlations is made available for others to use (available at: http:www.wwbp.org/).

Background

This section outlines recent work linking language with personality, gender, and age. In line with the focus of this paper, we predominantly discuss works which sought to gain psychological *insights*. However, we also touch on increasingly popular attempts at *predicting* personality from language in social media, which, for our study, offer an empirical means to compare a *closed vocabulary* analysis (relying on *a priori* word category human judgments) and an *open vocabulary* analysis (not relying on *a priori* word category judgments).

Personality refers to the traits and characteristics that make an individual unique. Although there are multiple ways to classify traits, we draw on the popular Five Factor Model (or "Big 5"), which classifies personality traits into five dimensions: *extraversion* (e.g., outgoing, talkative, active), *agreeableness* (e.g., trusting, kind, generous), *conscientiousness* (e.g., self-controlled, responsible, thorough), *neuroticism* (e.g., anxious, depressive, touchy), and *openness* (e.g., intellectual, artistic, insightful). With work beginning over 50 years ago and journals dedicated to it, the *FFM* is a well-accepted construct of personality.

131

Automatic Lexical Analysis of Personality, Gender, and Age

By examining what words people use, researchers have long sought a better understanding of human psychology. As Tauszczik & Pennebaker put it:

Language is the most common and reliable way for people to translate their internal thoughts and emotions into a form that others can understand. Words and language, then, are the very stuff of psychology and communication.

The typical approach to analyzing language involves counting word usage over pre-chosen categories of language. For example, one might place words like 'nose', 'bones', 'hips', 'skin', 'hands', and 'gut' into a *body* lexicon, and count how often words in the lexicon are used by *extraverts* or *introverts* in order to determine who talks about the body more. Of such word-category lexica, the most widely used is Linguistic Inquiry and Word Count or *LIWC*, developed over the last couple decades by human judges designating categories for common words. The 2007 version of *LIWC* includes 64 different categories of language ranging from part-of-speech (i.e. *articles, prepositions, past-tense verbs, numbers,...*) to topical categories (i.e. *family, cognitive mechanisms, affect, occupation, body,...*), as well as a few other attributes such as total number of words used.

Pennebaker & King conducted one of the first extensive applications of *LIWC* to personality by examining words in a variety of domains including diaries, college writing assignments, and social psychology manuscript abstracts. Their results were quite consistent across such domains, finding patterns such as *agreeable* people using more articles, *introverts* and those low in *conscientiousness* using more words signaling distinctions, and *neurotic* individuals using more negative emotion words. Mehl et al. tracks the natural speech of 96 people over two days. They found similar results to Pennebaker & King and that *neurotic* and *agreeable* people tend to use more first-person singulars, people low in *openness* talk more about social processes, *extraverts* use longer words.

The recent growth of online social media has yielded great sources of personal discourse. Besides advantages due to the size of the data, the content is often personal and describes everyday concerns. Furthermore, previous research has suggested populations for online studies and Facebook are quite representative. Sumner et al. examined the language of 537 Facebook users with *LIWC* while Holtgraves studied the text messages of 46 students. Findings from these studies largely confirmed past links with LIWC but also introduced some new links such as *neurotics* using more acronyms or those high in *openness* using more quotations.

The larger sample-sizes from social media also enabled the first study exploring personality as a function of single-word use. Yarkoni investigated LIWC categories along with single words in connection with Big-5 scores of 406 bloggers. He identified single word results which would not have been caught with *LIWC*, such as 'hug' correlating positively with *agreeableness* (there is no physical affection category in *LIWC*), but, considering the sparse nature of words, 406 blogs does not result in comprehensive view. For example, they find only 13 significant word correlations for *conscientiousness* while we find thousands even after Bonferonni-correcting significance levels. Additionally, they did not control for age or gender although they reported roughly 75% of their subjects were female. Still, as the most thorough point of comparison for *LIWC* results with personality,

Analogous to a personality construct, work has been done in psychology looking at the latent dimensions of self-expression. Chung and Pennebaker factor analyzed 119 adjectives used in student essays of "who you think you are" and discovered 7 latent dimensions labeled such as "sociability" or "negativity". They were able to relate these factors to the Big-5 and found only weak relations, suggesting 7 dimensions as an alternative construction. Later, Kramer and Chung ran the same method over 1000 unique words across Facebook status updates, finding three components labeled, "positive events", "informal speech", and "school". Although their vocabulary size was somewhat limited, we still see these as previous examples of open-vocabulary language analyses for psychology – no assumptions were made on the categories of words beyond part-of-speech.

LIWC has also been used extensively for studying gender and age. Many studies have focused on function words (articles, prepositions, conjunctions, and pronouns), finding females use more first-person singular pronouns, males use more articles, and that older individuals use more plural pronouns and future tense verbs. Other works have found males use more formal, affirmation, and informational words, while females use more social interaction, and deictic language. For age, the most salient findings include older individuals using more positive emotion and less negative emotion words, older individuals preferring fewer self-references (i.e. 'I', 'me') , , and stylistically there is less use of negation. Similar to our finding of 2000 topics (clusters of semantically-related words), Argamon et al. used factor analysis and identified 20 coherent components of word use to link gender and age, showing male components of language increase with age while female factors decrease.

Occasionally, studies find contradictory results. For example, multiple studies report that emoticons (i.e. ':)' ':-(') are used more often by females , , , but Huffaker & Calvert found males use them more in a sample of 100 teenage bloggers . This particular discrepancy could be sample-related – differing demographics or having a non-representative sample (Huffaker & Calvert looked at 100 bloggers, while later studies have looked at thousands of twitter users) or it could be due to differences in the domain of the text (blogs versus twitter). One should always be careful generalizing new results outside of the domain they were found as language is often dependent on context. In our case we explore language in the broad context of Facebook, and do not claim our results would up under other smaller or larger contexts. As a starting point for reviewing more psychologically meaningful language findings, we refer the reader to Tauszczik & Pennebaker's 2010 survey of computerized text analysis.

Eisenstein et al. presented a sophisticated *open-vocabulary* language analysis of demographics. Their method views language analysis as a multi-predictor to multi-output regression problem, and uses an L1 norm to select the most useful predictors (i.e. words). Part of their motivation was finding interpretable relationships between individual language features and sets of outcomes (demographics), and unlike the many predictive works we discuss in the next section, they test for significance of relationships between individual language features and outcomes. To contrast with our approach, we consider features and outcomes individually (i.e. an "L0 norm"), which we think is more ideal for our goals of explaining psychological variables (i.e. understanding openness by the words that correlate with it). For example, their method may throwout a word which is strongly predictive for only one outcome or which is collinear with other words, while we want to know all the words most-predictive for a given outcome. We also explore other types of *open-vocabulary* language features such as phrases and topics.

Similar language analyses also occurred in many fields outside of psychology or demographics. For example, Monroe et al. explored a variety of techniques that compare two frequencies of words – one number for each of two groups. In particular, they explored frequencies across democratic versus republican speeches and settled on a Bayesian model with regularization and shrinkage based on priors of word use. Lastly, Gilbert finds words and phrases that distinguish communication up or down a power-hierarchy across 2044 Enron emails. They used penalized logistic regression to fit a single model using coefficients of each feature as their "power"; this produces a good single predictive model but also means

136

words which are highly collinear with others will be missed (we run a separate regression for each word to avoid this).

Perhaps one of the most comprehensive language analysis surveys outside of psychology is that of Grimmer & Stewart. They summarize how automated methods can inexpensively allow systematic analysis and inference from large political text collections, classifying types of analyses into a class of hierarchy. Additionally, they provide cautionary advice; In relation to this work, they note that dictionary methods (such as the closed-vocabulary analyses discussed here) may signal something different when used in a new domain (for example 'crude' may be a negative word in student essays, but be neutral in energy industry reports: 'crude oil'). For comprehensive surveys on text analyses across fields see Grimmer & Stewart, O'Connor, Bamman, & Smith, and Tausczik & Pennebaker.

Predictive Models based on Language
In contrast with the works seeking to gain *insights* about psychological variables, research focused on *predicting* outcomes have embraced data-driven approaches. Such work uses open-vocabulary linguistic features in addition to *a priori* lexicon based features in predictive models for tasks such as stylistics/authorship attribution –, emotion prediction , , interaction or flirting detection, or sentiment analysis. In other works, ideologies of political figures (i.e. conservative to liberal) have been predicted based on language using supervised techniques or unsupervised inference of ideological space. Sometimes these works note the highest weighted features, but with their goal

137

being predictive accuracy, those features are not tested for significance and they usually are not the most individually distinguishing pieces of language. To elaborate, most approaches to prediction penalize the weights of words that are highly collinear with other words as they fit a single model per outcomes across all words. However, these highly collinear words which are suppressed could have revealed important insights with an outcome. In other words, these predictive models answer the question "what is the best combination of words and weights to predict personality?" whereas we believe answering the following question is best for revealing new insights: "what words, controlled for gender and age, are individually most correlated with personality?"

Recently, researchers have started looking at personality prediction. Early works in personality prediction used dictionary-based features such as *LIWC*. Argamon et al. (2005) noted that personality, as detected by categorical word use, was supportive for author attribution. They examined language use according to the traits of *neuroticism* and *extraversion* over approximately 2200 student essays, while focused on using function words for the prediction of gender. Mairesse et al. used a variety of lexicon-based features to predict all Big-5 personality traits over approximately 2500 essays as well as 90 sets of individual spoken words. As a first pass at predicting personality from language in Facebook, Golbeck used *LIWC* features over a sample of 167 Facebook volunteers as well as profile information and found limited success of a regression model. Similarly, Kaggle held a competition of personality prediction over Twitter messages, providing participants with language cues based on *LIWC*. Results of the competition suggested personality is difficult to predict based on language in social media, but it is not clear whether such a conclusion would have been drawn had *open-vocabulary* language cues been supplied for prediction.

In the largest previous study of language and personality, Iacobelli, Gill, Nowson, and Oberlander attempted prediction of personality for 3,000 bloggers. Not limited to categorical language they found open-vocabulary features, such as bigrams, to be better predictors than *LIWC* features. This motivates our exploration of open-vocabulary features for psychological insights, where we examine multi-word phrases (also called n-grams) as well as open-vocabulary category language in the form of automatically clustered groups of semantically related word (*LDA topics*, see "Linguistic Feature Extraction" in the "Materials and Methods" section). Since the application of Iacobelli's et al work was content customization, they focused on prediction rather than exploration of language for psychological insight. Our much larger sample size lends itself well to more comprehensive exploratory results.

Similar studies have also been undertaken for age and gender prediction in social media. Because gender and age information is more readily available, these studies tend to be larger. Argamon et al. predicted gender and age over 19,320 bloggers, while Burger et al. scaled up the gender prediction over 184,000 Twitter authors by using automatically guessed gender based-on gender-specific keywords in profiles. Most recently, Bamman et al. looked at gender as a function of language and social network statistics in twitter. They particularly looked at the characteristics of those whose gender was incorrectly predicted and found greater gender homophily in the social networks of such individuals.

These past studies, mostly within the field of computer science or specifically computational linguistics, have focused on prediction for tasks such as content personalization or authorship attribution. In our work, predictive models of personality, gender, and age provide a quantitative means to compare various *open-vocabulary* sets of features with a *closed-vocabulary* set. Our primary concern is to explore the benefits of an *open-vocabulary* approach for gaining *insights*, a goal that is at least as import as prediction for psychosocial fields. Most works for gaining language-based insights in psychology are *closed-vocabulary* (for examples, see previous section), and while many works in computational linguistics are open-vocabulary, they rarely focus on insight. We introduce the term "open-vocabulary" to distinguish an approach like ours from previous approaches to gaining *insight*, and in order to encourage others seeking insights to consider similar approaches. "Differential language analysis" refers to the particular process, for which we are not aware of another name, we use in our *open-vocabulary*.

Contributions
The contributions of this paper are as follows:

- First, we present the largest study of personality and language use to date. With just under 75,000 authors, our study covers an order-of-magnitude more people and instances of language features than the next largest study. The size of our data enables qualitatively different analyses, including open vocabulary analysis, based on more comprehensive sets of language features such as *phrases* and automatically derived *topics*. Most prior studies used *a priori* language categories, presumably due in part to the sparse nature of words and their relatively small samples of people. With smaller data sets, it is difficult to find statistically significant differences in language use for anything but the most common words.

- Our *open-vocabulary* analysis yields further insights into the behavioral residue of personality types beyond those from *a priori* word-category based approaches, giving unanticipated results (correlations between language and personality, gender, or age). For example, we make the novel discoveries that mentions of an assortment of social sports and life activities (such as *basketball, snowboarding, church, meetings*) correlate with *emotional stability*, and that *introverts* show an interest in Japanese media (such as *anime, pokemon, manga* and Japanese emoticons: ^_^). Our inclusion of phrases in addition to words provided further insights (e.g. that males prefer to precede 'girlfriend' or 'wife' with the possessive 'my' significantly more than females do for 'boyfriend' or 'husband'. Such correlations provide quantitative evidence for strong links between behavior, as revealed in language use, and psychosocial variables. In turn, these results suggest undertaking studies, such as directly measuring participation in activities in order to verify the link with emotional stability.

- We demonstrate open-vocabulary features contain more information than *a priori* word-categories via their use in predictive models. We take model accuracy in out-of-sample prediction as a measure of information of the features provided to the model. Models built from words and phrases as well as those from automatically generated topics achieve significantly higher out-of-sample prediction accuracies than standard lexica for each variable of interest (*gender*, *age*, and *personality*). Additionally, our prediction model for gender yielded state-of-the-art results for predictive models based entirely on language, yielding an out-of-sample accuracy of 91.9%.

- We present a word cloud visualization which scales words by correlation (i.e., how well they predict the given psychological variable) rather than simply scaling by frequency. Since we find thousands of significantly correlated words, visualization is key, and our *differential* word clouds provide a comprehensive view of our results.

- Lastly, we offer our comprehensive *word*, *phrase*, and *topic* correlation data for future research experiments (see: http://wwbp.org).

Materials and Methods

142

Ethics Statement

All research procedures were approved by the University of Pennsylvania Institutional Review Board. Volunteers agreed to written informed consent.

In seeking insights from language use about personality, gender, and age, we explore two approaches. The first approach, serving as a replication of the past analyses, counts word usage over manually created *a priori* word-category lexica. The second approach, termed *DLA*, serves as our main method and is *open-vocabulary* – the words and clusters of words analyzed are determined by the data itself.

Closed Vocabulary: Word-Category Lexica

A common method for linking language with psychological variables involves counting words belonging to manually-created categories of language. Sometimes referred to as the *word-count* approach, one counts how often words in a given category are used by an individual, the percentage of the participants' words which are from the given category:

$$p\,(category \mid subject) = \frac{\sum\limits_{word \in category} freq\,(word,\ subject)}{\sum\limits_{word \in vocab\,(subject)} freq\,(word,\ subject)}$$

where $freq\,(word, subject)$ is the number of the times the participant mentions $word$ and $vocab\,(subject)$ is the set of all words mentioned by the subject.

We use ordinary least squares regression to link word categories with author attributes, fitting a linear function between explanatory variables (*LIWC* categories) and dependent variables (such as a trait of personality, e.g. extraversion). The coefficient of the target explanatory variable (often referred to as β) is taken as the strength of relationship. Including other variables allows us to adjust for covariates such as gender and age to provide the unique effect of a given language feature on each psychosocial variable.

Open Vocabulary: Differential Language Analysis
Our technique, *differential language analysis* (*DLA*), is based on three key characteristics. It is

1. *Open-vocabulary* – it is not limited to predefined word lists. Rather, linguistic features including words, phrases, and topics (sets of semantically related words) are automatically determined from the texts. (I.e., it is "data-driven".) This means *DLA* is classified as a type of open-vocabulary approach.
2. *Discriminating* – it finds key linguistic features that distinguish psychological and demographic attributes, using stringent significance tests.
3. *Simple* – it uses simple, fast, and readily accepted statistical techniques.

We depict the components of this approach, and describe the three steps: 1) linguistic feature extraction, 2) correlational analysis, and 3) visualization in the following sections.

144

1. Linguistic Feature Extraction

We examined two types of linguistic features: a) *words and phrases*, and b) *topics*. *Words and phrases* consisted of sequences of 1 to 3 words (often referred to as 'n-grams' of size 1 to 3). What constitutes a word is determined using a tokenizer, which splits sentences into tokens ("words"). We built an emoticon-aware tokenizer on top of Pott's "happyfuntokenizer" allowing us to capture emoticons like '<3' (a heart) or ':-)' (a smile), which most tokenizers incorrectly divide up as separate pieces of punctuation. When extracting phrases, we keep only those sequences of words with high informative value according to point wise mutual information (PMI) [69], [70], a ratio of the joint-probability to the independent probability of observing the phrase:

$$pmi\,(phrase) = \log \frac{p(phrase)}{\Pi_{w \in phrase} p(w)}$$

In practice, we kept phrases with pmi values greater than $2 * length$, where $length$ is the number of words contained in the phrase, ensuring that phrases we do keep are informative parts of speech and not just accidental juxtapositions. All word and phrase counts are normalized by each subject's total word use ($p(word \mid subject)$), and we apply the Anscombe transformation to the normalized values for variance stabilization (p_{ans}):

$$p(phrase \mid subject) = \frac{freq\,(phrase,\,subject)}{\sum\limits_{phrase' \in vocab(subject)} freq\,(phrase',\,subject)}$$

$$p_{ans}(phrase \mid subject) = 2\sqrt{p(phrase \mid subject) + 3/8}$$

where $vocab(subject)$ returns a list of all words and phrases used by that subject. These Anscombe

145

transformed "relative frequencies" of words or phrases (p_{Ans}) are then used as the independent variables in all our analyses. Lastly, we restrict our analysis to those words and phrases which are used by at least 1% of our subjects, keeping the focus on common language.

The second type of linguistic feature, *topics*, consists of word clusters created using Latent Dirichlet Allocation (LDA). The LDA generative model assumes that documents (i.e. Facebook messages) contain a combination of topics, and that topics are a distribution of words; since the words in a document are known, the latent variable of topics can be estimated through Gibbs sampling. We use an implementation of the LDA algorithm provided by the Mallet package, adjusting one parameter ($alpha = 0.30$) to favor fewer topics per document, since individual Facebook status updates tend to contain fewer topics than the typical documents (newspaper or encyclopedia articles) to which LDA is applied. All other parameters were kept at their default. An example of such a model is the following sets of words (*tuesday, monday, wednesday, friday, thursday, week, sunday, saturday*) which clusters together days of the week purely by exploiting their similar distributional properties across messages.

To use topics as features, we find the probability of a subject's use of each topic:

$$p(topic \mid subject) = \sum_{word \in topic} p(topic \mid word) * p(word \mid subject)$$

where $p(word \mid subject)$ is the normalized word use by that subject and $p(topic \mid word)$ is the probability of the

146

topic given the word (a value provided from the LDA procedure). The prevalence of a word in a topic is given by $p(topic, word)$, and is used to order the words within a topic when displayed.

2. Correlational Analysis

Similar to word categories, distinguishing open-vocabulary words, phrases, and topics can be identified using ordinary least squares regression. We again take the coefficient of the target explanatory variable as its correlation strength, and we include other variables (e.g. age and gender) as covariates to get the unique effect of the target explanatory variable. Since we explore many features at once, we consider coefficients significant if they are less than a Bonferroni-corrected two-tailed P of 0.001. (I.e., when examining 20,000 features, a passing p-value is less than 0.001 divided by 20,000 which is $5 * 10^{-8}$).

Our correlational analysis produces a comprehensive list of the most distinguishing language features for any given attribute, *words, phrases,* or *topics* which maximally discriminate a given target variables. For example, when we correlate the target variables geographic elevation with language features ($N = 18,383$, $p < 0.001$, adjusted for gender and age), we find 'beach' the most distinguishing feature for low elevation localities, and 'the mountains' to be among the most distinguishing features for high elevation localities, (i.e., people in low elevations talk about the beach more, whereas people at high elevations talk about the mountains more). Similarly, we find the most distinguishing topics to be *(beach, sand, sun, water, waves, ocean, surf, sea, toes, sandy, surfing, beaches, sunset, Florida, Virginia)* for low elevations and *(Colorado, heading, headed, leaving, Denver, Kansas, City, Springs, Oklahoma, trip, moving, Iowa, KC, Utah, bound)* for high elevations. Others have looked at geographic location.

3. Visualization

An analysis over tens of thousands of language features and multiple dimensions results in hundreds of thousands of statistically significant correlations. Visualization is thus critical for their interpretation. We use word clouds to intuitively summarize our results. Unlike most word clouds, which scale word size by their frequency, we scale word size according to the strength of the correlation of the word with the demographic or psychological measurement of interest, and we use color to represent frequency over all subjects; that is, larger words indicate stronger correlations, and darker colors indicate more frequently used words. This provides a clear picture of which words and phrases are most discriminating while not losing track of which ones are the most frequent. Word clouds scaled by frequency are often used to summarize news, a practice that has been critiqued for inaccurately representing articles. Here, we believe the word cloud is an appropriate visualization because the individual words and phrases we depict in it are the actual results we wish to summarize. Further, scaling by correlation coefficient rather than frequency gives clouds that distinguish a given outcome.

Word clouds can also used to represent distinguishing topics. In this case, the size of the word within the topic represents its prevalence among the cluster of words making up the topic. We use the 6 most distinguishing topics and place them on the perimeter of the word clouds for *words and phrases*. This way, a single figure gives a comprehensive view of the most distinguishing words, phrases, and topics for any given variables of interest.

To reduce the redundancy of results, we automatically prune language features containing information already provided by a feature with higher correlation. First, we sort language features in order of their correlation with a target variable (such as a personality trait). Then, for phrases, we use frequency as a proxy for informative value, and only include additional phrases if they contain more informative words than previously included phrases with matching words. For example, consider the phrases 'day', 'beautiful day', and 'the day', listed in order of correlation from greatest to least; 'Beautiful day' would be kept, because 'beautiful' is less frequent than 'day' (i.e., it is adding informative value), while 'the day' would be dropped because 'the' is more frequent than 'day' (thus it is not contributing more information than we get from 'day'). We do a similar pruning for topics: A lower-ranking topic is not displayed if more than 25% of its top 15 words are also contained in the top 15 words of a higher ranking topic. These discarded relationships are still statistically significant, but removing them provides more room in the visualizations for other significant results, making the visualization as a whole more meaningful.

Word clouds allow one to easily view the features most correlated with polar outcomes; we use other

149

visualizations to display the variation of correlation of language features with continuous or ordinal dependent variables such as age. A standard time-series plot works well, where the horizontal axis is the dependent variable and the vertical axis represents the standard score of the values produced from feature extraction. When plotting language as a function of age, we fit first-order LOESS regression lines to the age as the x-axis data and standardized frequency as the y-axis data over all users. We are able to adjust for gender in the regression model by including it as a covariate when training the LOESS model and then using a neutral gender value when plotting.

Data Set: Facebook Status Updates

Our complete dataset consists of approximately 19 million Facebook status updates written by 136,000 participants. Participants volunteered to share their status updates as part of the *My Personality* application, where they also took a variety of questionnaires. We restrict our analysis to those Facebook users meeting certain criteria: They must indicate English as a primary language, have written at least 1,000 words in their status updates, be less than 65 years (to avoid the non-representative sample above 65), and indicate both gender and age (for use as controls). This resulted in $N = 74,941$ volunteers, writing a total of 309 million words (700 million feature instances of words, phrases, and topics) across 15.4 million status updates. From this sample each person wrote an average of 4,129 words over 206 status updates, and thus 20 words per update. Depending on the target variable, this number slightly varies as indicated in the caption of each result.

150

The personality scores are based on the International Personality Item Pool proxy for the NEO Personality Inventory Revised (NEO-PI-R). Participants could take 20 to 100 item versions of the questionnaire, with a retest reliability of $\alpha > 0.80$. With the addition of gender and age variables, this resulted in seven total dependent variables studied in this work. Personality distributions are quite typical with means near zero and standard deviations near 1. The statuses ranged over 34 months, from January 2009 through October 2011. Previously, profile information (i.e. network metrics, relationship status) from users in this dataset have been linked with personality, but this is the first use of its status updates.

Results

Results of our analyses over gender, age, and personality are presented below. As a baseline, we first replicate the commonly used *LIWC* analysis on our data set. We then present our main results, the output of our method, *DLA*. Lastly, we explore empirical evidence that *open-vocabulary* features provide more information than those from an *a priori* lexicon through use in a predictive model.

Closed Vocabulary

Figure 2 shows the results of applying the *LIWC* lexicon to our dataset, along side-by-side with the most comprehensive previous studies we could find for *gender*, *age*. and *personality*. In our case, correlation results are βvalues from an ordinary least squares linear regression where we can adjust for gender and age to give the unique effect of the target variable. One should keep in

151

mind that it is often found that effect sizes tend to be relatively smaller as sample sizes increase and become more stable.

Even though the previous studies listed did not look at Facebook, a majority of the correlations we find agree in direction. Some of the largest correlations emerge for the LIWC *articles* category, which consists of determiners like 'the', 'a', 'an' and serves as a proxy for the use of more nouns. Articles are highly predictive of males, being older, and *openness*. As a content-related language variable, the *anger* category also proved highly predictive for *males* as well as younger individuals, those low in *agreeableness* and *conscientiousness*, and high in *neuroticism*. *Openness* had the least agreement with the comparison study; roughly half of our results were in the opposite direction from the prior work. This is not too surprising since *openness* exhibits the most variation across conditions of other studies (for examples, see), and its component traits are most loosely related.

Open Vocabulary

Our *DLA* method identifies the most distinguishing language features (*words, phrases*: a sequence of 1 to 3 words, or *topics*: a cluster of semantically related words) for any given attribute. Results progress from a one variable proof of concept (gender), to the multiple variables representing age groups, and finally to all 5 dimensions of personality.

Language of Gender.

Gender provides a familiar and easy to understand proof of concept for open-vocabulary analysis. Figure 3 presents word clouds from age-adjusted gender correlations. We scale word size according to the strength of the relation and we use color to represent overall frequency; that is, larger words indicate stronger correlations, and darker colors indicate frequently used words. For the *topics*, groups of semantically-related words, the size indicate the relative prevalence of the word within the cluster as defined in the methods section. All results are significant at Bonferroni-corrected $p < 0.001$.

Many strong results emerging from our analysis align with our *LIWC* results and past studies of gender. For example, females used more emotion words (e.g., 'excited'), and first-person singulars, and they mention more psychological and social processes (e.g., 'love you' and '<3' –a heart). Males used more swear words, object references (e.g., 'xbox' and swear words).

Other results of ours contradicted past studies, which were based upon significantly smaller sample sizes than ours. For example, in 100 bloggers Huffaker et al. found males use more emoticons than females. We calculated power analyses to determine the sample size needed to confidently find such significant results. Since the Bonferonni-correction we use elsewhere in this work is overly stringent (i.e. makes it harder than necessary to pass significance tests), for this result we applied the Benjamini-Hochberg false discovery rate procedure for multiple hypothesis testing. Rerunning our language of gender analysis on reduced random samples of our

153

subjects resulted in the following number of significant correlations (Benjamini-Hochberg tested $p < 0.001$): 50 subjects: 0 significant correlations, 500 subjects: 7 correlations; 5,000 subjects: 1,489 correlations; 50,000 subjects: 13,152 correlations (more detailed results of power analyses across gender, age, and personality can be found in Figure S1). Thus, traditional study sample sizes, which are closer to 50 or 500, are not powerful enough to do data-driven DLA over individual words.

One might also draw insights based on the gender results. For example, we noticed 'my wife' and 'my girlfriend' emerged as strongly correlated in the male results, while simply 'husband' and 'boyfriend' were most predictive for females. Investigating the frequency data revealed that males did in fact precede such references to their opposite-sex partner with 'my' significantly more often than females. On the other hand, females were more likely to precede 'husband' or 'boyfriend' with 'her' or 'amazing' and a greater variety of words, which is why 'my husband' was not more predictive than 'husband' alone. Furthermore, this suggests the male preference for the possessive 'my' is at least partially due to a lack of talking about others' partners.

Language of Age

Figure 4 shows the word cloud (center) and most discriminating topics (surrounding) for four age buckets chosen with regard to the distribution of ages in our sample (Facebook has many more young people). We see clear distinctions, such as use of slang, emoticons, and Internet speak in the youngest group (e.g. ':)', 'idk', and a couple *Internet speak* topics) or work appearing in the 23

154

to 29 age group (e.g. 'at work', 'new job', as a *job position* topic). We also find subtle changes of topics progressing from one age group to the next. For example, we see a *school* related topic for 13 to 18 year olds (e.g. 'school', 'homework', 'ugh'), while we see a *college* related topic for 19 to 22 year olds (e.g. 'semester', 'college', 'register'). Additionally, consider the *drunk* topic (e.g. 'drunk', 'hangover', 'wasted') that appears for 19 to 22 year olds and a more reserved *beer* topic (e.g. 'beer', 'drinking', 'ale') for 23 to 29 year olds.

In general, we find a progression of school, college, work, and family when looking at the predominant topics across all age groups. *DLA* may be valuable for the generation of hypotheses about life span developmental age differences. Figure 5A shows the relative frequency of the most discriminating topic for each age group as a function of age. Typical concerns peak at different ages, with the topic concerning relationships (e.g. 'son', 'daughter', 'father', 'mother') continuously increasing across life span. On a similar note, Figure 5C shows 'we' increases approximately linearly after the age of 22, whereas 'I' monotonically decreases. We take this as a proxy for social integration, suggesting the increasing importance of friendships and relationships as people age. Figure 5B reinforces this hypothesis by presenting a similar pattern based on other social topics. One limitation of our dataset is the rarity of older individuals using social media; we look forward to a time in which we can track fine-grained language differences across the entire lifespan.

155

A. Standardized frequency for the best topic for each of the 4 age groups. Grey vertical lines divide groups: 13 to 18 (black: $n = 25,467$ out of $N = 74,859$), 19 to 22 (green: $n = 21,687$), 23 to 29 (blue: $n = 14,656$), and 30+ (red: $n = 13,049$). Lines are fit from first-order LOESS regression controlled for gender. **B.** Standardized frequency of social topic use across age. **C.** Standardized 'I', 'we' frequencies across age.

Language of Personality

We created age and gender-adjusted word clouds for each personality factor based on around 72 thousand participants with at least 1,000 words across their Facebook status updates, who took a Big Five questionnaire.

Figure 6 shows word clouds for extraversion and neuroticism. (See Figure S2 for openness, conscientiousness, and agreeableness.) The dominant words in each cluster were consistent with prior lexical and questionnaire work. For example, extraverts were more likely to mention social words such as 'party', 'love you', 'boys', and 'ladies', whereas introverts were more likely to mention words related to solitary activities such as 'computer', 'Internet', and 'reading'. In the openness cloud, words such as 'music', 'art', and 'writing' (i.e., creativity), and 'dream', 'universe', and 'soul' (i.e., imagination) were discriminating.

Topics were also found reflecting similar concepts as the words, some of which would not have been captured with *LIWC*. For example, although *LIWC* has socially related categories, it does not contain a *party* topic, which emerges as a key distinguishing feature for extraverts. Topics related to other types of social events are listed elsewhere, such as a sports topic for low neuroticism (emotional stability). Additionally, <u>Figure 6</u> shows the advantage of having phrases in the analysis to get clearer signal: e.g. people high in neuroticism mentioned 'sick of', and not just 'sick'.

While many of our results confirm previous research, demonstrating the instrument's face validity, our word clouds also suggest new hypotheses. For example, <u>Figure 6</u> (bottom-right) shows language related to emotional stability (low neuroticism). Emotionally stable individuals wrote about enjoyable social activities that may foster greater emotional stability, such as 'sports', 'vacation', 'beach', 'church', 'team', and a *family time* topic. Additionally, results suggest that introverts are interested in Japanese media (e.g. 'anime', 'manga', 'japanese', Japanese style emoticons: ^_^, and an *anime* topic) and that those low in *openness* drive the use of shorthands in social media (e.g. '2day', 'ur', 'every 1'). Although these are only language correlations, they show how *open-vocabulary* analyses can illuminate areas to explore further.

Predictive Evaluation

Here we present a quantitative evaluation of open-vocabulary and closed vocabulary language features. Although we have thus far presented subjective evidence that open-vocabulary features contribute more information, we hypothesize empirically that the inclusion of open-vocabulary features leads to prediction accuracies above and beyond that of closed-vocabulary. We randomly sampled 25% of our participants as test data, and used the remaining 75% as training data to build our predictive models.

We use a linear support vector machine (*SVM*) for classifying the binary variable of gender, and ridge regression for predicting age and each factor of personality. Features were first run through principal component analysis to reduce the feature dimension to half of the number of users. Both SVM classification and ridge regression utilize a regularization parameter, which we set by validation over the training set (we defined a small validation set of 10% of the training set which we tested various regularization parameters over while fitting the model to the other 90% of the training set in order to select the best parameter). Thus, the predictive model is created without any outcome information outside of the training data, making the test data an out-of-sample evaluation.

As open-vocabulary features, we use the same units of language as *DLA*: *words and phrases* (n-grams of size 1 to 3, passing a collocation filter) and *topics*. These features are outlined precisely under the "Linguistic Feature Extraction" section presented earlier. As explained in that section, we use Anscombe transformed relative frequencies of *words and phrases* and the conditional probability of a *topic* given a subject. For closed vocabulary features, we use the *LIWC* categories of language calculated as the relative frequency of a user mentioning a word in the category given their total word usage. We do not provide our models with anything other than these language usage features (independent variables) for prediction, and we use usage of all features (not just those passing significance tests from *DLA*).

As shown in Table 2, we see that models created with *open vocabulary* features significantly ($p < 0.01$) outperformed those created based on *LIWC* features. The *topics* results are of particular interest, because these automatically clustered word-category lexica were not created with any human or psychological data – only knowing what words occurred in messages together. Furthermore, we see that a model which includes *LIWC* features on top of the *open-vocabulary words*, *phrases*, and *topics* does not result in any improvement suggesting that the open-vocabulary features are able to capture predictive information which fully supersedes *LIWC*.

For personality we saw the largest relative improvement between *open-vocabulary* approaches and *LIWC*. Our best personality R score of 0.42 fell just above the standard "correlational upper-limit" for behavior to predict personality (a Pearson correlation of 0.3 to 0.4). Some researchers have discretized the personality scores for prediction, and classified people as being high or low (one standard deviation above or below the mean or top and bottom quartiles, throwing out the middle) in each trait. When we do such an approach, our scores are in similar ranges to such literature: 65% to 79% classification accuracy. Of course, such a high/low model cannot directly be used for classifying unlabeled people as one would also need to know who fits in the middle. Regression is a more appropriate predictive task for continuous outcomes like age and personality, even

159

though *R*scores are naturally smaller than binary classification accuracies.

We ran additional tests to evaluate only those words and phrases, topics, or *LIWC* categories that are selected via differential language analysis rather than all features. Thus, we used only those language features that significantly correlated (Bonferonni-corrected $p < 0.001$) with the outcome being predicting. To keep consistent with the main evaluation, we used no controls, and so one could view this as a univariate feature selection over each type of feature independently. We again found significant improvement from using the open-vocabulary features over *LIWC* and no significant changes in accuracy overall. These results are presented in Table S2.

In addition to demonstrating the greater informative value of *open-vocabulary* features, we found our results to be state-of-the-art. The highest previous *out-of-sample* accuracies for gender prediction based *entirely* on language were 88.0% over twitter data while our classifiers reach an accuracy of *91.9%*. Our increased performance could be attributed to our set of language features, a strong predictive algorithm (the support vector machine), and the large sample of Facebook data.

Discussion

Online social media such as Facebook are a particularly promising resource for the study of people, as "status" updates are self-descriptive, personal, and have emotional content. Language use is objective and quantifiable behavioral data, and unlike surveys and questionnaires, Facebook language allows researchers to observe

160

individuals as they freely present themselves in their own words. *Differential language analysis (DLA)* in social media is an unobtrusive and non-reactive window into the social and psychological characteristics of people's everyday concerns.

Most studies linking language with psychological variables rely on *a priori* fixed sets of words, such as the *LIWC* categories carefully constructed over 20 years of human research. Here, we show the benefits of an *open-vocabulary* approach in which the words analyzed are based on the data itself. We extracted *words*, *phrases*, and *topics* (automatically clustered sets of words) from millions of Facebook messages and found the language that correlates most with gender, age, and five factors of personality. We discovered insights not found previously and achieved higher accuracies than *LIWC* when using our *open-vocabulary* features in a predictive model, achieving state-of-the-art accuracy in the case of gender prediction.

Exploratory analyses like *DLA* change the process from that of testing theories with observations to that of data-driven identification of new connections. Our intention here is not a complete replacement for *closed-vocabulary* analyses like *LIWC*. When one has a specific theory in mind or a small sample size, an *a priori* list of words can be ideal; in an open-vocabulary approach, the concept one cares about can be drowned out by more predictive concepts. Further, it may be easier to compare static *a priori* categories of words across studies. However, automatically clustering words into coherent topics allows one to potentially discover categories that might not have been anticipated (e.g. sports teams, kinds of outdoor exercise, or Japanese cartoons). Open-vocabulary approaches also save labor in creating categories. They consider all words encountered and thus are able to adapt well to the evolving language in social media or other genres. They are also transparent in that the exact words driving correlations are not hidden behind a level of abstraction. Given lots of text and dependent variables, an open-vocabulary approach like *DLA* can be immediately useful for many areas of study; for example, an economist contrasting sport utility with hybrid vehicle drivers, a political scientist comparing democrats and republicans, or a cardiologist differentiating people with positive versus negative outcomes of heart disease.

Like most studies in the social sciences, this work is still subject to sampling and social desirability biases. Language connections with psychosocial variables are often dependent on context. Here, we examined language in a large sample of the broad context of Facebook. Under different contexts, it is likely some results would differ. Still, the sample sizes and availability of demographic information afforded by social media bring us closer to a more ideal representative sample. Our current results have face validity (subjects in high elevations talk about 'the mountains'), tie in with other research (neurotic people disproportionately use the phrase 'depressed'), suggest new hypotheses (an active life implies emotional stability), and give detailed insights (males prefer to precede 'wife' with the possessive 'my' more so than females precede 'husband' with 'my').

162

Over the past one-hundred years, surveys and questionnaires have illuminated our understanding of people. We suggest that new multipurpose instruments such as *DLA* emerging from the field of computational social science shed new light on psychosocial phenomena.

*****

Criminal profiling is more often known as "offender profiling" within law enforcement circles. I want to include an article from Wikipedia that is actually quite good.

Offender Profiling
http://en.wikipedia.org/wiki/Offender_profiling

Offender profiling, also known as **criminal profiling**, is a behavioral and investigative tool that is intended to help investigators to accurately predict and profile the characteristics of unknown criminal subjects or offenders. Offender profiling is also known as criminal profiling, criminal personality profiling, criminological profiling, behavioral profiling or criminal investigative analysis. Geographic profiling is another method to profile an offender. Television shows such as *Law & Order: Criminal Intent*, *Profiler* in the 1990s, the 2005 television series *Criminal Minds*, the 2011 one season television series *Criminal Minds: Suspect Behavior*, and the 1991 film *The Silence of the Lambs* have lent many names to what the FBI calls "criminal investigative analysis." Or the BAU (Criminal Minds)

163

Holmes and Holmes (2008) outline the three main goals of criminal profiling:

- The first is to provide law enforcement with a social and psychological assessment of the offender;
- The second goal is to provide law enforcement with a "psychological evaluation of belongings found in the possession of the offender" (p. 10);
- The third goal is to give suggestions and strategies for the interviewing process.

Ainsworth (2001) identified that there are four main approaches to offender profiling:

- The geographical approach, in which the patterns are analyzed in regard to timing and location of the crime scene, in order to determine where the offender lives and works
- Investigative psychology, this approach focuses on the use of psychological theories of analysis to determine the characteristics of the offender by looking at the presented offending behavior and style of offense
- The typological approach looks at the specific characteristics of the crime scene to then categorize the offender according to the various 'typical' characteristics
- The clinical approach to offender profiling in which the understanding of psychiatry

and clinical psychology is used to determine whether the offender is suffering from mental illness of various psychological abnormalities.

5 Procedural steps in generating a profile:

- 1. A thorough analysis of the type/nature of the criminal act is made and it is then compared to the types of people who have committed similar crimes in the past
- 2. An in depth analysis of the actual crime scene is made
- 3. The victim's background and activities are analyzed, to look for possible motives and connections
- 4. The possible factors for the motivation of the crime are analyzed
- 5. The description of the possible offender is developed, founded on the detected characteristics, which can be compared to with previous cases

In modern criminology, offender profiling is generally considered the "third wave" of investigative science:

- the first wave was the study of clues, pioneered by Scotland Yard in the 19th century;
- the second wave was the study of crime itself (frequency studies and the like);
- this third wave is the study of the psyche of the criminal.

Definitions

Offender profiling is a method of identifying the perpetrator of a crime based on an analysis of the nature of the offense and the manner in which it was committed. Various aspects of the criminal's personality makeup are determined from his or her choices before, during, and after the crime. This information is combined with other relevant details and physical evidence, and then compared with the characteristics of known personality types and mental abnormalities to develop a practical working description of the offender.

Psychological profiling may be described as a method of suspect identification which seeks to identify a person's mental, emotional, and personality characteristics (as manifested in things done or left at the crime scene). This was used in the investigation of the serial murders committed by Ted Bundy. Dr. Richard B. Jarvis, a psychiatrist with expertise on the criminal mind, predicted the age range of Bundy, his sexual psychopathy, and his above average intellect.

A further, more detailed example of how psychological profiling may be performed is the investigation of Gary Leon Ridgway, also known as the Green River Killer. This case also demonstrates the potential for incorrect predictions. John E. Douglas, an investigator who worked for the FBI, provided a twelve-page profile, which stated the suspect was:

- Probably a white male who had a dysfunctional relationship with women.

166

- Organized since he tried to hide the bodies and appeared to spend some time at the river
- Cunning in using rocks to weigh the victims down in the water to conceal them.
- Very mobile with a vehicle.
- Going to kill again.
- Like other serial killers, he would be prone to contacting police wanting to help in the investigations.

However, the profile created for Ridgway also revealed characteristics that did not apply to him, such as being an outdoorsman and being incapable of closeness to other people. Ridgway was not an outdoorsman, but frequented the Green River with one of his wives, and also had a very close relationship with his last wife, which contradicted the point in the profile of being incapable of closeness.

One type of criminal profiling is referred to as linkage analysis. Gerard N. Labuschagne (2006) defines linkage analysis as "a form of behavioral analysis that is used to determine the possibility of a series of crimes as having been committed by one offender." Gathering many aspects of the offender's crime pattern such as modus operandi, ritual or fantasy-based behaviors exhibited, and the signature of the offender help to establish a basis for a linkage analysis. An offender's modus operandi is his or her habits or tendencies during the killing of the victim. An offender's signature is the unique similarities in each of his or her kills. Mainly, linkage analysis is used when physical evidence, such as DNA, cannot be collected.

Labuschagne states that in gathering and incorporating these aspects of the offender's crime pattern, investigators must engage in five assessment procedures: (1) obtaining data from multiple sources; (2) reviewing the data and identifying significant features of each crime across the series; (3) classifying the significant features as either MO and/or ritualistic; (4) comparing the combination of MO and ritual/fantasy-based features across the series to determine if a signature exists; and (5) compiling a written report highlighting the findings.

History

The origins of profiling can be traced back to as early as the Middle Ages, with the inquisitors trying to "profile" heretics. Jacob Fries, Cesare Lombroso, Alphonse Bertillon, Hans Gross and several others realized the potential of profiling in the 19th century although their research is generally considered to be prejudiced, reflecting the biases of their time.

In 1912, a psychologist in Lackawanna, New York delivered in lecture in which he analyzed an unknown criminal who was suspected of having murdered a local boy named Joey Joseph. Based on the postcards which had been used to taunt the Lackawanna Police and the Joseph family, the profile ultimately led to the arrest and conviction of J. Frank Hickey.

A version of profiling is thought to have been used in the 1940s, when investigations relied on mental health professionals to create a profile of an offender in order to aid the police investigation. Soon after, as discussed

168

below, James Brussel was called upon to analyze the information on the Mad Bomber in New York City, and he created an accurate profile of the offender. This caught the attention of the FBI, who then worked to develop a technique for profiling, based on the process used by Brussel.

Notable profilers

Thomas Bond

During the 1880s, Thomas Bond, a medical doctor, tried to profile the personality of Jack the Ripper. Bond, a police surgeon, assisted in the autopsy of Mary Kelly. In his notes, dated November 10, 1888, he mentioned the sexual nature of the murders coupled with elements of apparent misogyny and rage. Dr. Bond also tried to reconstruct the murder and interpret the behavior pattern of the offender: soon he came up with a profile or signature personality traits of the offender to assist police investigation. The profile said that five murders of seven in the area at the time the report was written had been committed by one person alone who was physically strong, composed, and daring. The unknown offender would be quiet and harmless in appearance, possibly middle-aged, and neatly attired, probably wearing a cloak to hide the bloody effects of his attacks out in the open. He would be a loner, without a real occupation, eccentric, and mentally unstable. He might even suffer from a condition called Satyriasis, a sexual deviancy that is today referred to as hypersexuality or promiscuity. Bond also mentioned that he believed the offender had no anatomical knowledge and could not be a surgeon or

169

butcher. Moreover, Dr. Bond later concluded that the same offender was responsible for the murder of Alice McKenzie.

- Example of what Dr. Thomas Bond's First Profile of Jack the Ripper was:

"The murderer must have been a man of physical strength and great coolness and daring...subject to periodic attacks of homicidal and erotic mania. The characters of the mutilations indicate that the man may be in a condition sexually, that may be called Satyriasis"

Walter C. Langer

In 1943, Major General William J. Donovan, chief of the US Office of Strategic Services (OSS), asked Dr. Walter C. Langer, a psychoanalyst based in Boston, to develop a "profile" of Adolf Hitler. What the OSS wanted was a behavioral and psychological analysis of how Hitler might behave if the war turned against him.

Dr. Langer used speeches, Hitler's book Mein Kampf, interviews with people who had known Hitler, and some four hundred published works to complete his wartime report, which was eventually declassified by OSS and published by Langer (along with certain collateral material) as The Mind of Adolf Hitler in 1972. This work contains a profile of possible behavioral traits of Hitler, and his possible reactions to the idea of Germany losing World War II. Dr. Langer's profile noted that Hitler was meticulous, conventional, and prudish about his appearance and body. He was robust and viewed himself as a standard-bearer and trendsetter. He had manic phases, yet took little exercise. Due to a lack of evidence, Langer believed that Hitler was in reasonably good health, so it was unlikely he would die from natural causes, but he was deteriorating mentally. He would not try to escape to a neutral country, nor would he (in Langer's opinion) allow himself to be captured by the Allies. Hitler always walked diagonally from one corner to another when crossing a room, and he whistled a marching tune. He feared syphilis and germs.

Langer's profile also pointed out Hitler's oedipal complex, with the effect being the need to prove his manhood to his mother, and his masochistic coprolagnia and urolagnia. He detested the learned and the privileged, but enjoyed classical music, vaudeville, and Richard Wagner's opera. He showed strong streaks of sadism and liked circus acts that were risky and dangerous. He tended to speak in long monologues rather than have conversations. He had difficulty establishing close relationships with anyone. Since he appeared to be delusional, it was possible that his psychological structures would collapse in the face of imminent defeat. The most likely scenario was that he would commit suicide, although there was a possibility that he would order a henchman to perform euthanasia.

James A. Brussel

Between 1940 and 1956, a serial bomber terrorized New York City by planting bombs in public places including movie theaters, phone booths, Radio City Music Hall, Grand Central Terminal, and Pennsylvania Station. In

171

1956, the frustrated police requested a profile from Greenwich Village psychiatrist James A. Brussel, who was New York State's assistant commissioner of mental hygiene. Dr. Brussel studied photographs of the crime scenes and analyzed the so-called "mad bomber's" mail to the press. Soon he came up with a detailed description of the offender. In his profile, Dr. Brussel suggested that the unknown offender would be a heavy middle-aged man who was unmarried, but perhaps living with a sibling. Moreover, the offender would be a skilled mechanic from Connecticut, who was a Roman Catholic immigrant and, while having an obsessional love for his mother, would harbor a hatred for his father. Brussel noted that the offender had a personal vendetta against Consolidated Edison, the city's power company; the first bomb targeted its 67th Street headquarters. Dr. Brussel also mentioned to the police that, upon the offender's discovery, the "chances are he will be wearing a double-breasted suit. Buttoned."

From his profile, it was obvious to the police that the mysterious bomber would be a disgruntled current or unhappy former employee of Con Ed. The profile helped police to track down George Metesky in Waterbury, Connecticut; he had worked for Con Ed in the 1930s. He was arrested in January 1957 and confessed immediately. The police found Brussel's profile most accurate when they met the heavy, single, Catholic, and foreign-born Metesky. When the police told him to get dressed, he went to his bedroom and returned wearing a double-breasted suit, fully buttoned, just as Dr. Brussel had predicted. However, Malcolm Gladwell has written that offender profiling is not a science at all, but is couched in

172

such ambiguous language that it can support almost any interpretation; and about Brussel says:

Brussel did not really understand the mind of the Mad Bomber. He seems to have understood only that, if you make a great number of predictions, the ones that were wrong will soon be forgotten, and the ones that turn out to be true will make you famous. The Hedunit is not a triumph of forensic analysis. It's a party trick.

Dr. Brussel assisted New York City police from 1957 to 1972 and profiled many crimes, including murder. Dr. Brussel also worked with other investigative agencies. Brussel's profile led the Boston Police to the apprehension of Albert DeSalvo, the notorious serial sex murderer known as the Boston Strangler. The media dubbed Dr. Brussel as "Sherlock Holmes of the Couch".

Howard Teten

Howard D. Teten, a veteran police officer from California, joined the FBI in 1962. He was appointed as an instructor in applied criminology at the old National Police Academy in Washington, D.C. Teten was greatly interested in the application of offender profiling, and had included some of the ideas in his applied criminology course. He met Dr. Brussel and exchanged investigative ideas and psychological strategies in profiling crimes. Although Teten disagreed with Dr. Brussel's Freudian interpretations, he accepted other tenets of his investigative analysis.

In 1972 the FBI's Behavioral Science Unit at Quantico was formed, with Teten joining FBI Instructor Patrick J. Mullany's team. Teten and Mullany designed a method for analyzing unknown offenders in unsolved cases. The idea was to look at the behavioral manifestations at a crime scene for evidence of mental disorders and other personality traits, thus aiding the detectives' deductive reasoning. Their ideas on offender profiling were tested when a seven-year-old girl was abducted from a Rocky Mountains campsite in Montana in June 1973. The girl was abducted from a tent in the early hours; the offender overpowered her before she could alert her parents, who were sleeping nearby. When an intensive search for the missing child failed, the case was referred to the FBI.

Teten, Mullany and Col. Robert K. Ressler employed their criminal investigative analysis technique to track down the unknown offender. Their profile declared that the abductor was most likely a young, white, male, homicidal Peeping Tom; a sex killer who mutilates his victim after death, who sometimes takes body parts as souvenirs. Later, the profile led to the arrest of David Meirhofer, a local 23-year-old single man who was also a suspect in another murder case. The search of his house unearthed "souvenirs"—body parts taken from both victims. Meirhofer was the first serial killer to be caught with the aid of the FBI's new investigative technique, called offender profiling or criminal investigative analysis. A decade later, the technique became a more sophisticated and systematic profiling tool known as the Criminal Investigative Analysis Program (CIAP).

Richard Walter and Bob Keppel

174

In 1974, homicide detective Robert D. Keppel used new methods of psychological profiling to investigate notorious serial killers Ted Bundy and the Green River Killer. He combined his field expertise with criminal psychologist Richard Walter. As a psychologist in Michigan's notorious prison system, Walter had interviewed over two thousand murderers, sex-offenders and serial killers. Walter began to see common threads among offenders and was able to group all killings and sex crimes into four distinct "subtypes": power-assertive, power-reassurance, anger-retaliatory, and anger-excitation or sadism. He was the first to develop a matrix using suspect pre-crime, crime and post-crime behaviors as a tool for investigation. Walter later co-founded the Vidocq society, an exclusive organization of forensic professionals who solve cold cases for law enforcement agencies, worldwide. Together, Keppel and Walter created the HITS (Hunter Integrated Telemetry System) database, which lists characteristics of violent crimes so that common threads can be investigated. They also published a leading scholarly article for the FBI and violent crime investigators all over the world: "Profiling Killers: A Revised Classification Model for Understanding Sexual Murder".

John Douglas and Robert Ressler

In 1978, after Howard Teten left the Behavioral Science Unit, John Douglas and Robert Ressler became pillars of offender profiling in the FBI. They spent much time studying convicted sex murderers and interviewing them, creating organized and disorganized typology, which is still in use today. Ressler was also responsible for the

175

founding of the National Center for Analysis of Violent Crime (NCAVC) and at least partially responsible for the establishment of VICAP. Their studies provide more information on the behavioral patterns, traits and characteristics of criminals which can then be added to the offender profiling program.

David Canter

In 1986, police forces across the south of England were struggling to find the *Railway Rapist* who was then renamed the *Railway Killer* after murdering a victim for the first time. Dr. David Canter, a psychologist and criminologist then from Surrey University, was invited to compose British crime's first offender profile. When John Duffy was later arrested, charged and convicted, it turned out 13 of Canter's 17 proclamations about the perpetrator were accurate. Profiling became commonplace in large-scale police searches afterwards. David Canter came up with an equation that summarizes the principal research question in profiling: $A \Rightarrow C$. Canter defines 'A' as representing all actions that occur in a crime or that are related to a crime; 'C' represents the characteristics of the offender; '$\Rightarrow$' represents the scientific modeling that allows for inferences to be established regarding the characteristics from the actions.

Phases of profiling

According to Gregg O. McCrary, the basic premise is that behavior reflects personality. In a homicide case, for example, FBI profilers try to collect the personality of the

176

offender through questions about his or her behavior at four phases:

1. **Antecedent:** What fantasy or plan, or both, did the murderer have in place before the act? What triggered the murderer to act some days and not others?
2. **Method and manner:** What type of victim or victims did the murderer select? What was the method and manner of murder: shooting, stabbing, strangulation or something else?
3. **Body disposal:** Did the murder and body disposal take place all at one scene, or multiple scenes?
4. **Post-offense behavior:** Is the murderer trying to inject himself into the investigation by reacting to media reports or contacting investigators?

A sexual crime is analyzed in much the same way (bearing in mind that homicide is sometimes a sexual crime), with the additional information that comes from a living victim. Professor David Canter is the pioneer of scientific offender profiling, developing the discipline of Investigative Psychology as a response to his dissatisfaction with the scientific bases for this activity. The IAIP of which Canter is President now seeks to set professional guidelines for practice and research in this area.

Another phase of criminal profiling (crime scene investigation) is case linkage. According to Brent E. Turvey, case linkage or linking analysis refers to the process of determining whether or not there are discrete connections between two or more previously unrelated cases through crime scene analysis. It involves establishing and comparing the physical evidence, victimology, crime scene characteristics, modus operandi (MO)-organized or disorganized typologies-, and signature behaviors between each of the cases under review. It has two purposes:

1. To assist law enforcement with the application of its finite resources by helping to establish where to apply investigative efforts
2. To assist the court in determining whether or not there is sufficient behavioral evidence to suggest a common scheme or plan in order to address forensic issues, such as whether similar crimes may be tried together or whether other crimes may be brought in as evidence.

With respect to behavioral evidence, case linkage efforts have most typically hinged on three concepts:

1. MO, modus operandi
2. Signature
3. victimology

Problems

There are major problems with offender profiling that have been identified.

Incorrect information from profiling can lead to false positives or false negatives. Investigators may find a suspect who appears to fit an incorrect profile and ignore or stop investigating other leads. For example, Richard

Jewell was wrongly investigated (and attacked in the media) following the Centennial Olympic Park bombing in Atlanta. This not only caused great distress to Jewell, but delayed identifying the true culprit, Eric Robert Rudolph. This was a false positive: the profile identified Jewell as the offender when in fact he was not. The opposite of the false positive is the false negative: the profile yields incorrect information which would cause investigators to ignore a suspect who is actually guilty. For example, in the Beltway sniper attacks, the offender profile indicated that the killer was probably a white male in his thirties from the DC area acting alone— in fact, the crimes were perpetrated by two black males, one of whom was 41 and the other 17 years old, from the west coast of the U.S.

The Peggy Hettrick murder case is controversial because it is the only documented case of an individual having been convicted due to a reversed engineered false profile and the erroneous testimony of the psychologist who developed the profile. In 1999, a jury convicted Timothy Masters of the 1987 killing of Peggy Hettrick. Masters spent over 9 years in a Colorado prison before his release on January 22, 2008. Timothy Masters was arrested and convicted of sexual murder based on the testimony of a forensic psychologist while the opinion of a Robert R. "Roy" Hazelwood, a retired FBI criminal investigative analyst was ignored. The forensic psychologist developed a psychological profile of a killer using narrative and drawings made by Masters to conclude that Masters' supposed fantasy was the motive and behavioral preparation for the sexual murder, regardless of the fact that the forensic psychologist knew that there was no direct or physical evidence linking Masters to the crime. The cautionary lesson in the Masters case is what happens when forensic psychologists advance opinions about criminal matters based on the extrapolation of academic research on psychological concepts involving sexual homicide cases and reject the opinions of professional criminal profilers who incorporate law enforcement analysis coupled with criminal evidentiary considerations into their work.

Some experts in criminal psychology such as Brent Turvey, as quoted by journalist Malcolm Gladwell in *The New Yorker* have questioned its scientific validity. Many profilers and FBI agents are not psychologists, and some researchers who looked at their work found methodological flaws.

Three psychologists from the Universities of Liverpool and Hull are questioning the basic presumption that you can draw conclusions about a person from a single instance of behaviour under such special circumstances. "The notion that particular configurations of demographic features can be predicted from an assessment of particular configurations of specific behaviors occurring in short-term, highly traumatic situations seems an overly ambitious and unlikely possibility. Thus, until such inferential processes can be reliably verified, such claims should be treated with great caution in investigations and should be entirely excluded from consideration in court."

Active profiling as allowed by the Department of Justice includes covert alteration of the environment to observe the responses of a suspect. This can be used to check whether the suspect's behavior fits the profile, but risks being labeled as police harassment or entrapment.

Popular use of the term *criminal profiler* has led to the proliferation of many self-described profilers offering their purported expert opinions on cable news shows in response to incidents capturing national attention in the United States. Such individuals usually have degrees in criminal justice or psychology but lack any law enforcement experience, or *vice versa.*

How To Protect Yourself on Social Media Sites

Cyber criminal activity is increasing at an exponential rate because it is the safest crime to commit. Cyber criminals know that committing cyber crimes below $50,000 are pretty much ignored by law enforcement. Law enforcement is in a big pickle here; it neither has the resources, budget, personnel or expertise to combat cyber crime and apprehend cyber criminals. Like it or not, each individual is left to protect themselves from the lurking cyber criminals and present the hardest target possible so they go off and attack a least prepared individual or business.

Areas of Personal EXPOSURE

- Credit Card Fraud
- Identity Theft
- Financial Scams
- Child Predation
- Computer Hijacking
- Malware
- Spyware
- Viruses
- Keystroke Logging
- Phishing
- User Account & Password Theft
- Cell Phone Spying
- Online Auction Fraud – Ebay, etc.
- And much more…

The above areas of personal exposure are the more prevalent forms of cyber crimes directed against individuals. It is by no means a complete list.

Be on the Lookout for…

Surfing the Web

One way that hackers get hold of you is when you surf the web. They put up enticing websites and as soon as you bring one up on your screen they are secretly downloading spyware onto your computer. Here are a few ways to protect yourself when web surfing:

Anonymizer: http://www.anonymizer.com/
Anonymouse:
http://www.anonymouse.org/anonwww.html
Identity Cloaker:
http://www.identitycloaker.com/?a_aid=neternatives
StartPage: https://www.startpage.com/
Tor Project: https://www.torproject.org/
Freenet Project: https://www.freenetproject.org/

You can also use various proxies to cloak your IP address:

Proxy Heaven: http://www.proxy-heaven.blogspot.com/
Proxy Services: http://www.proxyservices.com/
Your Private Proxy: http://www.yourprivateproxy.com/
HideMyAss: http://www.hidemyass.com/proxy-list/
MyPrivateProxy: http://www.myprivateproxy.net/

Cell Phone Spying

One of the easiest ways to become a victim of cyber-crime is by hacking into your cell phone and installing spyware. Today's Cell Phone spyware does not require that the hacker have possession of your phone. They simply call your cell phone number and whether it is answered or not, it takes all of about 30-seconds to marry your phone to the spyware.

Spyware of this type is readily available on the open market. Go here:
http://www.flexispy.com/?ref=1252800

Did you know that with the help of a simple, inexpensive device, anyone with access to your phone could read your private text messages (SMS), even if you have deleted them previously? This device can even recover contacts and a good number or previously dialed numbers. Go here:
http://www.brickhousesecurity.com/cellphone-spy-simcardreader.html

There is also a device that costs a whopping $20 that will tell you the cell phone number of any cell phone within 20-feet of the device. And "NO" we will not tell you where to get one or even what it is called.

The #1 Personal Intrusion is Cell Phone Spying

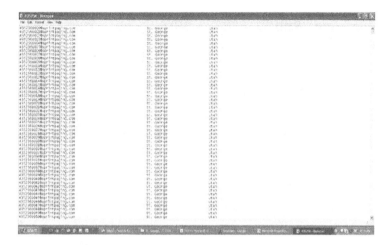

Where do hackers get your cell phone number? See below and the best part is that it is FREE!

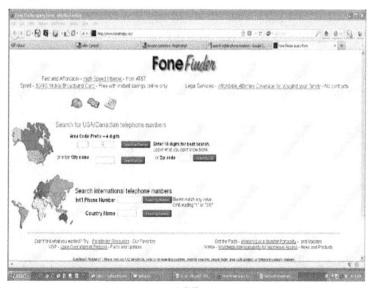

Cell Phone Spying Detection

Your Battery Temperature

One indicator of a possible phone tap is the temperature of your battery. Feel your cell phone if you haven't used it for a while. If it feels warm, this means your phone could be still in use, even if you are not on a call. Please note however that heat may be from overuse. Your battery being hot is only a potential sign if your phone has been powered down for a while.

Phone Not Staying Charged

Having to charge your cell phone more often than normal is another potential sign. If you haven't used it any more than usual, your phone could be in use when you aren't using it. When a cell phone is tapped it loses its battery life faster. A tapped cell phone is constantly recording conversations in the room, even when the phone appears to be idle. You can use an app like BatteryLife LX or Battery LED (iPhone) to monitor your phone's battery life and history over time.

[Note]: Cell phone batteries tend to lose the ability to stay charged over time. If you've had your phone for over a year, your battery may be going bad due to overuse and constant charging over time.

Delay in Shutting Down

When shutting down your phone, if you face issues such as a delay, the back light remaining lit for a time after being shut down, or refusal to shut off, your phone could be tapped. Always be aware of inexplicable activity on your phone. Since phones are made up of hardware and software, however, this could also be caused due to a glitch in the system or some kind of internal problem as well.

More Strange Activity
While turned on, does your phone ever light up, shut down, power up, or install a program on its own? Strange activity could also be a sign of someone else controlling your device.

Note that this can also happen due to interference during the transmission of data.

Background Noise
When on a call, a tapped phone will often include background noises. Usually in the form of echoes, static, or clicking, these sounds can either be caused by interference, a bad connection, or someone else listening in. If you ever hear a pulsating static noise coming from your phone when you are not using it, however, you may have a problem.

Distortion
If you are using your cell phone in close proximity to other electronic devices, like a television, and the other devices become distorted, this could be a sign that additional hardware is installed in the cell phone. A lot of times this distortion is normal, but if it is happening while you're not on a call it could be something to watch for.

What Can You Do About This?

For tips on what you can do if you are ever in this situation, as well as a visual display of some of the signs mentioned above, I invite you to watch this YouTube video entitled, "Is Your Cell Phone Bugged?":

http://www.youtube.com/watch?v=ujosfSkHFrQ

Email

Your email accounts can quite easily be hacked. There is software available on the open market that breaks usernames and passwords. Also, if your computer is hacked, most people leave sensitive information on their computer that can fall into a hacker's hands.

To protect your usernames and passwords use Roboform, which is 128-bit encrypted and virtually impossible to hack into:

http://www.roboform.com/php/pums/rfprepay.php?affid=ta556

You can also protect yourself by using a secure email service like Hushmail:

http://www.husmail.com

https://riseup.net/en

http://www.zoho.com/

https://www.hover.com/

Virtual Privacy Networks:

https://www.witopia.net/

https://www.privatvpn.se/en/

http://www.strongvpn.com

Identity Theft

Identity theft occurs when someone uses your personally identifying information, like your name, Social Security number, or credit card number, without your permission, to commit fraud or other crimes. The FTC estimates that as many as 9 million Americans have their identities stolen each year. In fact, you or someone you know may have experienced some form of identity theft.

The crime takes many forms. Identity thieves may rent an apartment, obtain a credit card, or establish a telephone account in your name. You may not find out about the theft until you review your credit report or a credit card statement and notice charges you didn't make—or until you're contacted by a debt collector.

Identity theft is serious. While some identity theft victims can resolve their problems quickly, others spend hundreds of dollars and many days repairing damage to their good name and credit record. Some consumers victimized by identity theft may lose out on job opportunities, or be denied loans for education, housing or cars because of negative information on their credit reports. In rare cases, they may even be arrested for crimes they did not commit.

How do thieves steal an identity?

Identity theft starts with the misuse of your personally identifying information such as your name and Social Security number, credit card numbers, or other financial account information. For identity thieves, this information is as good as gold. Skilled identity thieves may use a variety of methods to get hold of your information, including:

Dumpster Diving. They rummage through trash looking for bills or other paper with your personal information on it.

Skimming. They steal credit/debit card numbers by using a special storage device when processing your card.

Phishing. They pretend to be financial institutions or companies and send spam or pop-up messages to get you to reveal your personal information.

Changing Your Address. They divert your billing statements to another location by completing a change of address form.

Old-Fashioned Stealing. They steal wallets and purses; mail, including bank and credit card statements; pre-approved credit offers; and new checks or tax information. They steal personnel records, or bribe employees who have access.

190

Pretexting. They use false pretenses to obtain your personal information from financial institutions, telephone companies, and other sources.

What do thieves do with a stolen identity?

Once they have your personal information, identity thieves use it in a variety of ways.
Credit card fraud:

They may open new credit card accounts in your name. When they use the cards and don't pay the bills, the delinquent accounts appear on your credit report. They may change the billing address on your credit card so that you no longer receive bills, and then run up charges on your account. Because your bills are now sent to a different address, it may be some time before you realize there's a problem.

Phone or utilities fraud:

191

They may open a new phone or wireless account in your name, or run up charges on your existing account. They may use your name to get utility services like electricity, heating, or cable TV.

Bank/finance fraud:
They may create counterfeit checks using your name or account number. They may open a bank account in your name and write bad checks. They may clone your ATM or debit card and make electronic withdrawals your name, draining your accounts. They may take out a loan in your name.

Government documents fraud:
They may get a driver's license or official ID card issued in your name but with their picture. They may use your name and Social Security number to get government benefits. They may file a fraudulent tax return using your information.

Other fraud:
They may get a job using your Social Security number. They may rent a house or get medical services using your name. They may give your personal information to police during an arrest. If they don't show up for their court date, a warrant for arrest is issued in your name.

How can you find out if your identity was stolen?

The best way to find out is to monitor your accounts and bank statements each month, and check your credit report on a regular basis. If you check your credit report regularly, you may be able to limit the damage caused by identity theft.

Unfortunately, many consumers learn that their identity has been stolen after some damage has been done. You may find out when bill collection agencies contact you for overdue debts you never incurred. You may find out when you apply for a mortgage or car loan and learn that problems with your credit history are holding up the loan. You may find out when you get something in the mail about an apartment you never rented, a house you never bought, or a job you never held.

What should you do if your identity is stolen?

Filing a police report, checking your credit reports, notifying creditors, and disputing any unauthorized transactions are some of the steps you must take immediately to restore your good name.

Should you file a police report if your identity is stolen?

A police report that provides specific details of the identity theft is considered an Identity Theft Report, which entitles you to certain legal rights when it is provided to the three major credit reporting agencies or to companies where the thief misused your information. An Identity Theft Report can be used to permanently block fraudulent information that results from identity theft, such as accounts or addresses, from appearing on your credit report. It will also make sure these debts do not reappear on your credit reports. Identity Theft Reports can prevent a company from continuing to collect debts that result from identity theft, or selling them to others for collection. An Identity Theft Report is also needed to place an extended fraud alert on your credit report.

You may not need an Identity Theft Report if the thief made charges on an existing account and you have been able to work with the company to resolve the dispute. Where an identity thief has opened new accounts in your name, or where fraudulent charges have been reported to the consumer reporting agencies, you should obtain an Identity Theft Report so that you can take advantage of the protections you are entitled to.

In order for a police report to entitle you to the legal rights mentioned above, it must contain specific details about the identity theft. You should file an ID Theft Complaint with the FTC and bring your printed ID Theft Complaint with you to the police station when you file your police report. The printed ID Theft Complaint can be used to support your local police report to ensure that it includes the detail required.

A police report is also needed to get copies of the thief's application, as well as transaction information from companies that dealt with the thief.

Cyberstalking

Cyberstalking is the use of the Internet or other electronic means to stalk or harass an individual, a group of individuals, or an organization. It may include false accusations, monitoring, making threats, identity theft, damage to data or equipment, the solicitation of minors for sex, or gathering information in order to harass. The definition of "harassment" must meet the criterion that a reasonable person, in possession of the same information, would regard it as sufficient to cause another reasonable person distress. Cyberstalking is different from spatial or offline stalking. However, it sometimes leads to it, or is accompanied by it. When identifying cyberstalking and particularly when considering whether to report it to any kind of legal authority, the following features can be

195

considered to characterize a true stalking situation: malice, premeditation, repetition, distress, obsession, vendetta, no legitimate purpose, personally directed, disregarded warnings to stop, harassment, and threats.

A number of key factors have been identified:

False accusations. Many cyberstalkers try to damage the reputation of their victim and turn other people against them. They post false information about them on websites. They may set up their own websites, blogs or user pages for this purpose. They post allegations about the victim to newsgroups, chat rooms or other sites that allow public contributions, such as Wikipedia or Amazon.com.

Attempts to gather information about the victim. Cyberstalkers may approach their victim's friends, family and work colleagues to obtain personal information. They may advertise for information on the Internet, or hire a private detective. They often will monitor the victim's online activities and attempt to trace their IP address in an effort to gather more information about their victims.

Encouraging others to harass the victim. Many cyberstalkers try to involve third parties in the harassment. They may claim the victim has harmed the stalker or his/her family in some way, or may post the victim's name and telephone number in order to encourage others to join the pursuit.

False victimization. The cyberstalker will claim that the victim is harassing him/her. Bocij writes that this

196

phenomenon has been noted in a number of well-known cases.

Attacks on data and equipment. They may try to damage the victim's computer by sending viruses.

Ordering goods and services. They order items or subscribe to magazines in the victim's name. These often involve subscriptions to pornography or ordering sex toys then having them delivered to the victim's workplace.

Arranging to meet. Young people face a particularly high risk of having cyberstalkers try to set up meetings between them.

Types of Cyberstalkers

Of women
Harassment and stalking of women online is common, and can include rape threats and other threats of violence, as well as the posting of women's personal information. It is blamed for limiting victims' activities online or driving them offline entirely, thereby impeding their participation in online life and undermining their autonomy, dignity, identity and opportunities.

Of intimate partners
Cyberstalking of intimate partners is the online harassment of a current or former romantic partner. It is a form of domestic violence, and experts say its purpose is to control the victim in order to encourage social isolation and create dependency. Harassers may send repeated insulting or threatening e-mails to their victims, monitor

or disrupt their victims' e-mail use, and use the victim's account to send e-mails to others posing as the victim or to purchase goods or services the victim doesn't want. They may also use the internet to research and compile personal information about the victim, to use in order to harass her.

By anonymous online mobs

Web 2.0 technologies have enabled online groups of anonymous people to self-organize to target individuals with online defamation, threats of violence and technology-based attacks. These include publishing lies and doctored photographs, threats of rape and other violence, posting sensitive personal information about victims, e-mailing damaging statements about victims to their employers, and manipulating search engines to make damaging material about the victim more prominent. Victims are often women and minorities. They frequently respond by adopting pseudonyms or going offline entirely. A notable example of online mob harassment was the experience of American software developer and blogger Kathy Sierra. In 2007, a group of anonymous individuals attacked Sierra, threatening her with rape and strangulation, publishing her home address and Social Security number, and posting doctored photographs of her. Frightened, Sierra cancelled her speaking engagements and shut down her blog, writing "I will never feel the same. I will never be the same."

Experts attribute the destructive nature of anonymous online mobs to group dynamics, saying that groups with homogeneous views tend to become more extreme as members reinforce each other's beliefs, they fail to see themselves as individuals, so they lose a sense of personal responsibility for their destructive acts, they dehumanize their victims, which makes them more willing to behave destructively, and they become more aggressive when they believe they are supported by authority figures. Internet service providers and website owners are sometimes blamed for not speaking out against this type of harassment.

Corporate cyberstalking
Corporate cyberstalking is when a company harasses an individual online, or an individual or group of individuals harasses an organization. Motives for corporate cyberstalking are ideological, or include a desire for financial gain or revenge.

Perpetrators

Profile
Preliminary research has identified four types of cyberstalkers: the vindictive cyberstalkers noted for the ferocity of their attacks; the composed cyberstalker whose motive is to annoy; the intimate cyberstalker who attempts to form a relationship with the victim but turns on them if rebuffed; and collective cyberstalkers, groups with motive.

The general profile of the harasser is cold, with little or no respect for others. The stalker is a predator who can wait patiently until vulnerable victims appear, such as women or children, or may enjoy pursuing a particular person, whether personally familiar to them or unknown. The harasser enjoys and demonstrates their power to pursue and psychologically damage the victim.

Behaviors

Cyberstalkers find their victims by using search engines, online forums, bulletin and discussion boards, chat rooms, and more recently, through social networking sites, such as MySpace, Facebook, Bebo, Friendster, Twitter, and Indymedia, a media outlet known for self-publishing.

They may engage in live chat harassment or flaming or they may send electronic viruses and unsolicited e-mails. Cyberstalkers may research individuals to feed their obsessions and curiosity. Conversely, the acts of cyberstalkers may become more intense, such as repeatedly instant messaging their targets. More commonly they will post defamatory or derogatory statements about their stalking target on web pages, message boards and in guest books designed to get a reaction or response from their victim, thereby initiating contact. In some cases, they have been known to create fake blogs in the name of the victim containing defamatory or pornographic content.

When prosecuted, many stalkers have unsuccessfully attempted to justify their behavior based on their use of public forums, as opposed to direct contact. Once they get a reaction from the victim, they will typically attempt to track or follow the victim's internet activity. Classic cyberstalking behavior includes the tracing of the victim's IP address in an attempt to verify their home or place of employment.

Some cyberstalking situations do evolve into physical stalking, and a victim may experience abusive and excessive phone calls, vandalism, threatening or obscene mail, trespassing, and physical assault. Moreover, many physical stalkers will use cyberstalking as another method of harassing their victims.

Financial Fraud & Scams

Are There Anyways of Overcoming Cyber Fraud?

Internet is the fastest growing medium on earth that you would find these days and for everything it is the best solution that people consider looking into. Where it has all the benefits and advantages like communication, link building, advertisement, online movie downloads, online song downloads, emailing, instant messaging and searching out the concerns and issues there are plenty of things that internet has got wrong as well. There are multiple different kinds of internet scams and frauds that are out there that you have to be careful from. It is something that has been bothering individuals ever since internet was introduced and many times, simple things could make you a victim when you won't even get to know of it.

The email scam is at the top of the internet scams and internet fake activities. People have had a routine of making money from different resources. You might have been through those false emails and messages that come into your inbox saying you won a lottery or you just made thousands of dollars from some resource which you don't even know of. These cyber fraud emails are often auto generated and are sent out to hundreds of people like you so they could enter their account information and even simple money transactions for those people to take benefits from. After paying the processing fee to the scammed email, the individuals would get no suitable response to it and they would rather be asked for the bank account information and different sort of things that could lead the scam artists to the big amount of money and funds.

You can stop cyber fraud by reporting them to the local police and even to the online websites that have an option to do so. Most of the time, people don't consider reporting such things because they are considered unimportant; this is the main reason why scammers are getting more confidence towards what they are doing. One of the other causes due to which this cyber fraud is spreading day by day is because people overlook the cyber laws and regulations that are made out by the websites and forums. People should get to know more about internet laws and what to do once they find out someone is not abiding by them in an effective manner. One should take out significant amount of time checking the emails and several other notifications online to see which ones are valid and which ones aren't.

Cyber fraud refers to any type of deliberate deception for unfair or unlawful gain that occurs online. The most common form is online credit card theft. Other common forms of monetary cyber fraud include nondelivery of paid products purchased through online auctions and nondelivery of merchandise or software bought online. Cyber fraud also refers to data break-ins, identity theft, and cyberbullying, all of which are seriously damaging.

Here's an example: A 20-year-old Facebook user posted: *"I eyed this girl on campus for months before I finally got the nerve to talk to her. I created an excuse to ask her a question and then started chatting her up. I must have given off the vibe that I was interested because right away, she dropped the bomb that she had a boyfriend. Bummed but not discouraged, I got my computer-savvy friend to hack into her boyfriend's Facebook account and change his relationship status to 'single.' The girl must have freaked out because the next thing I heard, they'd gotten into a huge fight and broken things off. A few days later, I asked her about her boyfriend, totally playing it off like I had no idea they were through. When she told me what had happened, I offered to take her out for coffee to get her mind off the breakup. My plan worked, because after our little date, she came back to my dorm room and we hooked up."*

Not all cyber fraud occurs through e-mail, but most of them do. Other methods are on the Internet itself. You may even get a letter through the post, because your postal address may have been captured by a spyware program or spam e-mail you replied to with your postal address included in the reply. Most scams exploit people's greediness. There is always promise of great returns on money you should invest in them. You can stay safe by following common sense and a few basic simple rules:

- Never send people money that contacted you by e-mail, or any other method in the Internet, period. Especially if you never heard of them before. What clear minded person will send money to a complete stranger?
- Never reply to, or click on any links in e-mails requesting personal, account or any kind of user information.
- Never reply to, or click on any links in e-mails from organizations you are not member of. Why will Amazon, PayPal, eBay, Barclays Bank, or any organization send you e-mail if you are not a member of them?
- Never reply to, or click on any links in lottery or competition e-mails, you never entered. How can you suddenly win a competition you never entered?

Another way to identify fraud is looking at the real URL the link in the e-mail points to. How do I do that? Well most of the popular e-mail clients have a status bar at the bottom of your screen. If you hover with your mouse cursor above the link, the URL (Uniform Resource Locator, in other words, the exact web address it points to) will appear in the status bar. These links should point to the main domain of the company.

For instance the links in e-mail from PayPal should start with www.paypal.com, nothing else. If it starts with something like www.pay-pal.com, www.pay.pal.com, www.paypal_.com, www.paypalsecure.com or any variation of the real domain, then it's fraudulent, even if it points to a secure server (These links start with https:// and not the standard http://).

Any variation of the real domain points to a different server, not owned by PayPal, where you can get infected by viruses, spyware, adware, or become victim of a hacking attempt.

What is the #1 Internet Scam today?

U.S. Colleges and Universities Most Favored Target for Phishing

Phishing attacks against colleges and universities are focused on stealing the login credentials that students use to access all their personal university-related information and email; credentials that usually consist of students' usernames and passwords. Why phishers are seeking out students' information?

1. Young naïve girls ripe for cyberstalking and;
2. Application for financial aid or bogus student loans, as demonstrated by a recent case in Arizona.

Phishing attack masquerading as a University's Webmail portal

Phishing attack disguised as a University's login page

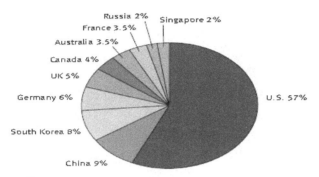

Top Ten Countries Hosting Phishing Attacks

Computer Hijacking

Computer Hijacking is a crime where the criminal takes over your computer and you are unable to control anything that is being done to your computer. This is a federal offence and the criminal will be jailed if caught.

How to protect against computer hijacking and against theft of your personal data (with potential to be used in Identity Theft).

Hijacking can only happen when hijacker's software finds its way to your computer. Identity theft comes with unauthorized access to your information.

So the best way to protect is:

Don't let them in!

Keep out software that you do not trust, *such as*:

- Any suspicious e-mail attachments
- Files downloaded from strange places
- ActiveX and Plugins from untrusted sites
- Use Spyware

To achieve this you need
- Several building blocks to be in place:
- Patch your browsers.
- Antivirus product.
- Anti spyware product.
- Personal firewall

You should look after your protection software:

- Keep them up-to-date.
- Check them regularly (for example - weekly) that automatic update is really working.
- Configure your software (like antivirus) to scan your computer daily (at night or at lunch time)

Keep software on your computers patched. Attackers would not be able to exploit known vulnerabilities and execute their programs through security holes.

To achieve that –

- Keep and maintain list of software you have installed
- Check for updates for each package regularly. Switch ON automatic checking for updates whenever it is possible.
- Note: Do you use MS Office? When did you check for MS Office update last time? Burn critical updates, Service Packs, Product Releases etc. on the two blank

CDs and store one on site and one off site. *List of what I think is critical for the current versions of Windows OS could be found on this site soon.*

Keep you data safe and available for restore in case that something does happen.

You will need your important information be available ASAP.

To achieve this -

- Identify data that should be preserved
- Keep your business related data files (such as drawings,
  plans, documents, presentations, program, schedules, lists of customers) in well identified places on your hard drive (or server)
- Check where is your e-mail program keeps your mail box and address book.
- Back up that data regularly.
- Check that backed up data can be restored correctly and actually used. Do it regularly
- Store back up media outside your main office.

This would help as part of any disaster. Power failure could destroy your hard drives. Thieves could steal your computers. You would need your data to keep business running.

So to make a conclusion:

Create the list what should be done and how often.
Check   that   it   is   achievable
Make schedule out of it. Put it in your dairy (electronic or
paper). Follow it
Review it when necessary.

Keystroke Logging - Phishing

Keystroke logging (often called **keylogging**) is the
action of tracking (or logging) the keys struck on a
keyboard, typically in a covert manner so that the person
using the keyboard is unaware that their actions are being
monitored. There are numerous keylogging methods,
ranging from hardware and software-based approaches to
electromagnetic and acoustic analysis.

Software-based keyloggers
A logfile from a software-based keylogger
A control window from a software-based keylogger
These are software programs designed to work on the
target computer's operating system. From a technical
perspective there are five categories:

Hypervisor-based: The keylogger can theoretically
reside in a malware hypervisor running underneath the
operating system, which remains untouched. It effectively
becomes a virtual machine. Blue Pill is a conceptual
example.

Kernel-based: This method is difficult both to write and
to combat. Such keyloggers reside at the kernel level and
are thus difficult to detect, especially for user-mode
applications. They are frequently implemented as rootkits

that subvert the operating system kernel and gain unauthorized access to the hardware, making them very powerful. A keylogger using this method can act as a keyboard device driver for example, and thus gain access to any information typed on the keyboard as it goes to the operating system.

API-based: These keyloggers hook keyboard APIs; the operating system then notifies the keylogger each time a key is pressed and the keylogger simply records it. Windows APIs such as GetAsyncKeyState, GetForegroundWindow, etc. are used to poll the state of the keyboard or to subscribe to keyboard events. These types of keyloggers are the easiest to write, but where constant polling of each key is required, they can cause a noticeable increase in CPU usage, and can also miss the occasional key. A more recent example simply polls the BIOS for pre-boot authentication PINs that have not been cleared from memory.

Form grabbing based: Form grabbing-based keyloggers log web form submissions by recording the web browsing onsubmit event functions. This records form data before it is passed over the Internet and bypasses HTTPS encryption.

Memory injection based: Memory Injection (MITB)-based keyloggers alter memory tables associated with the browser and other system functions to perform their logging functions. By patching the memory tables or injecting directly into memory, this technique can be used by malware authors who are looking to bypass Windows

UAC (User Account Control). The Zeus and Spyeye Trojans use this method exclusively.

Packet analyzers: This involves capturing network traffic associated with HTTP POST events to retrieve unencrypted passwords.

Remote access software keyloggers - These are local software keyloggers with an added feature that allows access to the locally recorded data from a remote location. Remote communication may be achieved using one of these methods:

- Data is uploaded to a website, database or an FTP server.
- Data is periodically emailed to a pre-defined email address.
- Data is wirelessly transmitted by means of an attached hardware system.

The software enables a remote login to the local machine from the Internet or the local network, for data logs stored on the target machine to be accessed.

Used by police - In 2000, the FBI used a keystroke logger to obtain the PGP passphrase of Nicodemo Scarfo, Jr., son of mob boss Nicodemo Scarfo. Also in 2000, the FBI lured two suspected Russian cyber criminals to the US in an elaborate ruse, and captured their usernames and passwords with a keylogger that was covertly installed on a machine that they used to access their computers in Russia. The FBI then used these credentials to hack into the suspects' computers in Russia in order to obtain evidence to prosecute them.

Countermeasures - The effectiveness of countermeasures varies, because keyloggers use a variety of techniques to capture data and the countermeasure needs to be effective against the particular data capture technique. For example, an on-screen keyboard will be effective against hardware keyloggers, transparency will defeat some screenloggers - but not all - and an anti-spyware application that can only disable hook-based keyloggers will be ineffective against kernel-based keyloggers.

Also, keylogger software authors may be able to update the code to adapt to countermeasures that may have proven to be effective against them.

Anti keyloggers - An anti keylogger is a piece of software specifically designed to detect keyloggers on your computer, typically comparing all files in your computer against a database of keyloggers looking for similarities which might signal the presence of a hidden keylogger. As anti keyloggers have been designed specifically to detect keyloggers, they have the potential to be more effective than conventional antivirus software; some antivirus software do not consider certain keyloggers a virus, as under some circumstances a keylogger can be considered a legitimate piece of software.

User Account – Password Theft

Use a password management program, which stores all of my passwords safely under one master password.

The key is to make sure you have a strong master password for your password management program to protect your list of passwords. You'll want to create strong passwords for each site that you log into as well.

A strong password must have at least 8 characters (the longer the better), with a mixture of upper and lower-case letters, numbers and, if the site or service allows, special characters, such as "!," "#" and "?." It should be something you can remember easily. A long sentence works well when you take the first letter of each word and then substitute the vowels for numbers or symbols.

For example: The quick brown fox jumped inside the orange box and slept = Tqbfj1t0b&s

Once you've created your master password, you can set up your password manager. It stores your passwords and user names in an encrypted database, enabling you to quickly access them. Once you have your password manager running, it fills in your user ID and password for you.

The free Mozilla Firefox Web browser for PCs and Macs has a built-in password manager, but you need to make sure you create a master password to protect your list. Other browsers — Internet Explorer, Safari and Chrome — can remember passwords for you, but they do not have a manager or master password to protect your passwords, so it's best to use a dedicated program.

For stand-alone password managers, one of the best is RoboForm Everywhere, which works with Macs and PCs, as well as iPhones and Android phones. The program can auto-fill just about any online form, including email, name, phone number and credit card information.

http://www.roboform.com/php/pums/rfprepay.php?affid=ta556

And for Macs (and PCs), check out 1Password ($49.95 at agilewebsolutions.com). The software saves passwords, credit card numbers, account registration information, just about anything you can think of, and auto-fills it all across most browsers on a Mac, including Safari, Firefox and Camino.

There's also an app for iPhone and iPad ($9.99 in iTunes) that will sync with your desktop and stop you from having to peck out your passwords on that tiny touchscreen keyboard.

Hard Drive & Disc Encryption
Hacking your hard drive and other data storage devices can be preventing by using a free disc encryption program called TrueCrypt:

http://www.truecrypt.org/docs/

TRUECRYPT
FREE OPEN-SOURCE ON-THE-FLY ENCRYPTION

TrueCrypt encrypts everything on your hard drive and all your personal information and is virtually impossible to bust into and hack.

Here are a few more encryption providers:

http://www.endoacustica.com/index_en.htm
http://www.hotspotshield.com/

Miscellaneous Protection

The Best Firewall: http://www.comodo.com/

Stop Unwanted Mail: https://www.catalogchoice.org/

Secure Mailing Address: http://www.earthclassmail.com/

Secure VOIP Phone: http://zfoneproject.com/

Secure Chat Room: https://crypto.cat/

You can review chat room logs using this: http://www.pimall.com/nais/chatstick.html#

You can detect PORN on any computer instantly:

http://www.pimall.com/nais/porndetectionstick.html#

Identify weaknesses and vulnerabilities in your personal computer:

http://www.eeye.com/products/retina/retina-network-scanner

Secure Search Engine

http://duckduckgo.com/

Privacy Apps for your browser

http://news.ghostery.com/
http://abine.com/dntdetail.php

I Have a Special Gift for My Readers

I appreciate my readers for without them I am just another author attempting to make a difference. If my book has made a favorable impression please leave me an honest review.   Thank you in advance for you participation.

My readers and I have in common a passion for the written word as well as the desire to learn and grow from books.

My special offer to you is a massive ebook library that I have compiled over the years. It contains hundreds of fiction and non-fiction ebooks in Adobe Acrobat PDF format as well as the Greek classics and old literary classics too.

In fact, this library is so massive to completely download the entire library will require over 5 GBs open on your desktop.

Use the link below and scan all of the ebooks in the library. You can select the ebooks you want individually or download the entire library.

The link below does not expire after a given time period so you are free to return for more books rather than clog your desktop. And feel free to give the link to your friends who enjoy reading too.

I thank you for reading my book and hope if you are pleased that you will leave me an honest review so that I can improve my work and or write books that appeal to your interests.

Okay, here is the link…

http://www.epubwealth.com/bookstore-bookstore-services/epubwealth-promotion-download-page/

PS: If you wish to reach me personally for any reason you may simply write to mailto:support@epubwealth.com.

I answer all of my emails so rest assured I will respond.

Meet the Author

Dr. Treat Preston is a behavioral scientist specializing in all types of relationships and associated problems, psychological triggers as applied to commercial advertising and marketing, and energy psychology. He is a best-selling author with numerous books dealing on publishing, behavioral science, marketing and more. He is also one of the lead research scientists with AppliedMindSciences.com, the mind research unit of ForensicsNation.com. As a Senior Forensics Investigator, Dr. Preston profiles perpetrators of all types of crimes and assists the ForensicsNation team of investigators in identifying and tracking down cyber criminals of all types all the way to apprehension and incarceration.

He and his wife Cynthia reside in Auburn, California.

Visit some of his websites
http://www.AddMeInNow.com
http://www.AppliedMindSciences.com
http://www.BookbuilderPLUS.com
http://www.BookJumping.com
http://www.EmailNations.com
http://www.EmbarrassingProblemsFix.com
http://www.ePubWealth.com
http://www.ForensicsNation.com
http://www.ForensicsNationStore.com
http://www.FreebiesNation.com
http://www.HealthFitnessWellnessNation.com
http://www.Neternatives.com
http://www.PrivacyNations.com

http://www.RetireWithoutMoney.org
http://www.SurvivalNations.com
http://www.TheBentonKitchen.com
http://www.Theolegions.org
http://www.VideoBookbuilder.com

Some Other Books You May Enjoy From ePubWealth.com, LLC Library Catalog

EPW Library Catalog Online
http://www.epubwealth.com/wp-content/uploads/2013/07/Leland-benton-private-turbo.pdf

EPW Library Catalog Download
http://www.filefactory.com/f/562ef3ea1a054f0a

www.ingramcontent.com/pod-product-compliance
Lightning Source LLC
Chambersburg PA
CBHW070944050326
40689CB00014B/3332